Contents

Editors' Notes

AS WE PROCEED in our efforts to further develop the profession of fundraising, it is important to remember that the process itself is really quite simple. Research clearly demonstrates that the most effective fundraising derives from personal contact by an individual who has a strong relationship with a potential donor. In reviewing the following more technical aspects in the book, it may be useful to examine them from this perspective.

This issue explores the impact of information technology on fundraising management—the operative term being *management*.

When we talk about technology management we are really talking about a change in human behavior in the workplace. For example, we wouldn't make a significant change in a manual filing system without first soliciting input from and involving those individuals using the system. The same process should also be observed when more technological aspects of the workplace are adjusted.

As a fundraising organization grows in terms of staff size and complexity of services, technological decisions are often outsourced or delegated to specialized individuals within the organization. Technically and economically, this may appear to be the best solution. However, too often the separation of technological decisions from direct line management and the end user may result in ineffective implementation of technology. This issue highlights the value of using a comprehensive involvement strategy when implementing various technologies in the workplace.

Smaller fundraising organizations challenged by technological advances are frequently more acutely impacted. Not only must they attempt to keep pace with the tools of other fundraising organizations, but they also must meet changing expectations of donors. E-mail, fax, cellular phones, computers, and other technologies create still more challenges for the management of these organizations.

NEW DIRECTIONS FOR PHILANTHROPIC FUNDRAISING, NO. 11, SPRING 1996 © JOSSEY-BASS PUBLISHERS

Throughout this issue, the use of technology to replace manual functions is addressed. We also discuss more complex ways that technologies function as value-adding tools in the fundraising process. For example, we discuss how data analysis obtained from advanced computing technologies can be used to focus an organization's efforts. In the past, we have frequently focused only on financial summary data rather than on behavioral and other interesting questions. These new ways of understanding our donors can enable organizations to more effectively address donors' interests and therefore potentially increase giving. Strategies to more effectively research individual donors through the use of technology are also addressed.

Additionally, we take a look at the frequently reported and discussed topic of the "Information Superhighway" and explore its impact on the fundraising process.

In Chapter One, Paul J. Matijevic addresses the challenges that face personnel when technology is introduced into the workplace. Matijevic gives useful pointers on how to deal with the fears and difficulties faced in developing and implementing an effective technology.

In Chapter Two, Michael O. Ranney provides an individual case description of a small nonprofit organization's efforts to implement a new technology system.

In Chapter Three, Dale A. DiSanto provides an overview of the way changes in technology lead to changes in fundraising infrastructure in an organization. DiSanto addresses personnel, training, and information needs in the development environment.

In Chapter Four, Deborah Strauss explores the linkages between on-line technologies and the fundraising office. Strauss reviews the functionality, the tools, and the risks of using telecommunications in professional fundraising.

In Chapter Five, Tim Mills-Groninger identifies and addresses important issues to consider when selecting fundraising software.

In Chapter Six, Laura J. Avery and John L. Gliha discuss developing a prospect research and management operation for the smaller nonprofit organization.

In Chapter Seven, Pamela J. O'Neil discusses developing a process to assure timely and effective reporting. O'Neil focuses on meeting the needs of fundraising staff, internal management, and external audiences.

We hope that this volume excites your interest in the advantages gained from active participation by both management and staff in the process of planning and implementing technology.

It is our aim in the following work to clearly indicate why strong and well-reasoned leadership in technological planning is critical to the overall success of an organization.

We appreciate the efforts of each of the contributing authors. We thank them for taking time away from their busy professional and personal lives to share their thoughts and experiences on the rapidly changing use of technology in development. We especially appreciate the work of Peter Westover, who has aided in the editing process greatly with his countless hours of trying to read our writing.

James D. Miller
Deborah Strauss
Editors

JAMES D. MILLER *is director of development for the Fisher College of Business at Ohio State University. He is on the faculty for the Fund Raising School at the Indiana University Center on Philanthropy.*

DEBORAH STRAUSS *is executive director of the nonprofit Information Technology Resource Center in Chicago, providing assistance with technology to nonprofit organizations. She is a long-term member of the National Society of Fund Raising Executives.*

Personnel face challenges when technology is introduced into the workplace. This chapter discusses the difficulties involved in developing and implementing an effective technology plan.

1

The human dimension and change concept: The impact of people interacting with technology

Paul J. Matijevic

> Change is inevitable. In a progressive country change is constant.
> —Benjamin Disraeli, *Oxford Dictionary of Quotations*

THERE IS NO CAREER PATH on the planet that has been unaffected by the technological revolution. Fundraising is no exception. We are living in the information age—technology is the present and the future—and for us to deny that fact is to deny reality. Critics of technology will argue that all fundraising can be done with a yellow pad and a pencil. This may have once been true, but is no longer the case. I am not saying that the established practices of face-to-face solicitation and direct mail are not integral components of any successful fundraising program. These elements, although in flux, provide a certain consistency to the profession. But in 1996 and in the years to come, skillful use of technology is and will continue to be as important as these constants. The sophisticated development

NEW DIRECTIONS FOR PHILANTHROPIC FUNDRAISING, NO. 11, SPRING 1996 © JOSSEY-BASS PUBLISHERS

office manages both donors and data with the utmost skill and with the most current techniques. For the fundraising professional, this means staying abreast of the latest thought in both solicitation and technology.

In every profession, one sees individuals who have grown to either fear or embrace the concept of technology as it applies to that field. In this article, I intend to explore some of the ways in which my colleagues have addressed their fears and learned to embrace the benefits of technology.

Fears

How many times have you heard the words "If it ain't broke, don't fix it"? People are often reluctant to change their methods, especially when the techniques they are currently applying have proven successful. It amazes me to see how staunch people become if you suggest to them that technology could improve or enhance their productivity. "We do not do things like that here," or "We could never afford that!" or "Why should we change when this way has worked for so long?" are three responses commonly given. I have encountered many people who are passive rather than proactive when they approach technology. They will do nothing—rather than seek new methods or applications that could enhance their efforts, these individuals will not take any initiative. Their attitude is best reflected in the statement, "What we don't know can't hurt us!" However, ignorance of the technology affecting one's field can no longer be used as an acceptable excuse. In a world where applications are being developed daily to enhance every facet of life, you owe it to yourself to become aware of what is available, and how it could help you do your job.

I believe that many people fear technology because they are not confident in their own learning capabilities. People who had difficulty in math or science in school or just don't have an aptitude for scientific subjects will quite naturally fear learning something so technically oriented as the computer. After all, logical thinking is critical to comprehension of computer concepts. Additionally, many development staff members have tremendous difficulty adapting to computerized methods because they are not provided with adequate training on use of both software and hardware. Organizations typically shortcut the training process, thinking they can spend money on the tools and disregard the cost of training. In some cases, organizations simply do not support their employees through the learning process. Every individual is unique, and the learning curve for each individual will be different. Lack of adequate training and lack of training that encompasses individual learning differences can compound the fears associated with learning something technically difficult, and will often create a situation that is quite difficult to overcome.

Employees in this situation develop a fear of failure. They doubt their own abilities in situations where they are forced to learn a computer system on their own, especially if the software is fairly complicated—and most development software packages are complex. When left in this situation, staff will become disheartened and critical of new products. Many times I have seen frustrated employees resort to business as usual; they simply resume record keeping and word processing in the manner they were accustomed to before the purchase of the new technology.

I have encountered a number of successful development officers who have come to view the computer with a certain amount of skepticism. They wonder how we can trust our wealth of information to a small machine and some software. They have not yet made the leap of faith—they don't yet believe that what you put in the computer will be retrievable. They need confidence in the person entering data and in the retrieval process in order to believe that the information they are receiving is valid and correct. I think there are many in the development field who are uncomfortable with this lack of control—they cannot overcome the inherent threat to their own omniscience. Those who believe that they alone are capable of remembering all the details about their donor base will never be comfortable in an environment where the storage and retrieval of information is controlled by the competence of a data entry person and the capabilities of a computer.

A few years ago, in one of my most frightening computer-related experiences, I encountered a senior level development professional who essentially told me that using a computer was below me. At this highly prestigious institution, senior level fundraisers do not have computers in their offices. Instead, they use yellow pads and have secretaries proficient in shorthand. I was amazed that this organization could raise so much money and yet had several senior level professionals who were computer illiterate—and admitted it. When I questioned one of them, he stated that the computers are for the secretaries. We are hired to raise money. When I replied with my beliefs about the essential need for computers and for officewide computer literacy, I was met with a blank stare.

I have also experienced development office environments where the belief persists that it is wasteful to devote human resources to managing information systems. This is a reflection of the "yellow pad and pencil" attitude—the idea that human resources should be devoted only to performing the accepted practices of raising money. This attitude does, however, raise a fair question: How much time and effort and energy should a development office devote to its information systems? There is an underlying question as well: In a society where fundraising has become so scientific, where donors expect fundraisers to have knowledge about their lives and giving history and personal interests, and in development offices where fundraisers must manage hundreds of prospects, is it realistic to think anyone can get by without an information system?

This is not an issue of becoming a slave to the computer or of having all your human resources devoted to data management, as some might suggest. Rather, this is an issue of implementing an effective system that will assist the fundraising process. The fear-of-slavery notion can more aptly be described as a fear of change. Development professionals cannot conduct business today as we did ten years ago and expect to be successful. Only by embracing technology and its benefits will we be successful in attaining our goals.

Enhancement to the organization and process

It is a major undertaking for a development office to commit to computerization. The psychological ramifications are far reaching, and many of the fears I have discussed previously do arise during the conversion process. But a fundraising staff must believe that a computer system will enhance their ability to raise money.

Once the decision about a system is made, and a system is installed, it will be obvious within a short period of time that the development staff is better informed about its constituency. This level of awareness is achieved in two ways: through the input of information, and through the decision-making process pertaining to the actual data entry.

As a development office rummages through files, reviews paper trails, coordinates post-it notes to the correct files, and actually goes through the process of physically entering data, the staff becomes more and more knowledgeable about its donor base. Any kind of general review of files like the one that occurs during a major data entry project enhances a staff's knowledge about its constituencies. Information such as name, address, phone number, giving history, personal affiliations, personal goals, relationships to other donors, board affiliations, and corporate affiliations are all trackable. This information is vital for good solicitation, and should be checked during the review and entry process for accuracy. Even though the review of all this information appears to be a daunting task, the result is an accurate data system that is easily accessible.

Standardizing the subsequent entry of data is crucial to continued accuracy. Once decisions are made as to how donors will be entered into a system, the procedure should remain constant to maintain continued accuracy. Preparation of a manual listing the standardized entry procedures for the organization is very helpful, especially if the office has high turnover.

Unfortunately, there is frequently some conflict about how to best store information. Those who practice the method of mentally tracking information resent those individuals who believe that computerization is superior. Arguably, a database and contact management system *is* better than note cards, legal pads, sticky notes stuffed in files, and people's memory.

I remember a situation I once experienced where a senior member of a development staff argued that he was capable of remembering all the information he needed regarding his 150 to 200 major gift prospects. His organization was considering a conversion from paper records to PC-based fundraising software. This individual publicly challenged colleagues who expressed the contrary belief: that one cannot possibly remember everything about prospects. The vast majority of the staff was in agreement that it was in the best interest of the organization to proceed with the data conversion. The organization went forward with the installation of the new computer system, against the senior professional's objections. After some time, it became evident that those fundraisers who used the data system were more effective in raising money than the resistant individual who opposed the system and refused to use it. Ultimately, it was revealed that this senior person was actually incapable of using the new computer system—principally because of an unwillingness to learn. He was computer illiterate and thought he could disguise the fact by focusing attention on his unique ability to recall information.

With all the personnel changes a typical development office experiences, how can it possibly be argued that a staff person's memory is the best storage place for information? Once again, I know that large sums of money have been raised with information tracked only by human memory. But I think the operative words in this statement are *have been*. Our business is not the same as it was fifteen years ago. We as development professionals cannot think that we can solicit the same way we used to. Having an easily accessed source of reliable information is critical for our success—databases and contact management software provide this easy access system.

Issues in the workplace

Every technological conversion raises new systems-related and personnel issues that, in many cases, are as new to an organization as the technology. The success of a conversion often depends on how well an organization can cope with these new issues. In this section I want to explore some of these topics and possible solutions that a nonprofit might use when facing these changes.

Training

Training is always a problem when an organization has a technology change. It is difficult to teach personnel about technology. People frequently fear a new system, which makes educating a staff that much more difficult. In many cases, staff is willing to learn, but an organization is not willing to teach. Financial resources are provided for the actual purchase and implementation of a new computer system, but not for training the staff on how to use the system.

It is also important for organizations to choose training programs that meet the needs of their employees. I have witnessed a situation where an organization installed a fairly sophisticated system, and hired the wrong person to train the staff. The newly hired trainer had computer skills—was versed in hardware and networks, and could reasonably discuss software. However, the trainer's communication skills were poor. After only a few sessions, it was obvious that this person could not meet the needs of the employees—in some cases, employees actually took over classes in order to more effectively communicate the information that the trainer was presenting. It was not a lack of technical skill on the part of the new employee; rather, this person could not phrase statements in such a way as to communicate coherent thoughts to the staff. Additionally, the trainer was very poor at answering questions, and often became upset when employees would ask very basic questions about the new software. Needless to say, the relationship between the organization and this employee did not last long.

I have also heard stories about new software or hardware being installed at organizations, with training sessions either never scheduled, or scheduled months after the installation. In one case, an organization bought an upgrade of a particular software package. Although this may not sound like a substantial change, in this instance it meant moving from DOS to Windows. The unfortunate part of this story was that the organization did not schedule official training on the Windows version of the application for over six months! This delay cost the organization in productivity because the staff spent most of that six-month period learning how to use the new application. The organization believed that since it was only an upgrade, training was not essential for the successful use of this application.

I think one can best describe this kind of behavior on the part of an organization as apathy. Management apathy, when it relates to something as important as training, sends the wrong message to employees. If an organization does not believe that training the employees on a new piece of software is important, how can it expect employees to use the software and try to implement changes in systemic processes with the help of the software? Additionally, employees read this lack of concern on the part of an organization as license to avoid or underuse the new purchase, especially when it requires changing office procedures. Why change, they think, when we do not know what we are hoping to achieve with this new system and have been successful in the past without it?

In my experience, it is critical for an organization to make these decisions simultaneously—purchase software (and hardware, if necessary) and purchase training to use it. Without that type of commitment on the part of an organization, the transition will not be easy, regardless of whether the change is as simple as an upgrade of software or as dramatic as a full replacement of the hardware and software used by an organization.

Skills for life

It is very important to discuss with staff the ramifications of any computer change. One major issue often overlooked is what I like to call skills for life. If we assume that computers will continue to dominate the workplace in the next twenty-five years, then any skills learned from on-the-job training can and will be used again as employees change jobs or career paths. For example, the employee who learned WordPerfect 5.0 or 5.1 in a first job is likely to be using WordPerfect 6.0 or 6.1 now. The skills learned from experience with the earlier release of WordPerfect were not wasted—only transferred. My own experience is very applicable as an example.

In my first development job, I gained the experience of working closely with a PC-based fundraising program. In one way or another I have been able to carry this experience to each position that I have since held. Most nonprofits have development offices; most development offices now have fundraising software or are contemplating the purchase of fundraising software. I have never worked in a development post where I have been unable to transfer my basic knowledge of database architecture and fundraising reporting to that environment—all gained from that first experience with a computer database.

Actually, most computer knowledge is transferable even if you change careers entirely. For most word processors, databases, and spreadsheets, the basic concepts remain the same—the only things that change are the particulars (that is, what keystrokes perform what functions).

Professional consultation

When an organization decides to make a computer transition, such as moving from DOS to Windows, from stand-alone personal computers to a network, or even from very old software to state-of-the-art technology, it is important for management to remain open to outside assistance with the transition. Many organizations, especially nonprofits, feel this is a waste of money. This is especially true in environments where there has been a history of tight funds, or where board members (or donors) feel that any outside assistance that has to be paid for is a frivolous waste of contributed income and that bringing an expert on board for such a conversion is unnecessary. Unfortunately, this thinking often costs organizations more money in the long term. The cost of hiring a consultant on a temporary basis to ensure an accurate, speedy, and seamless conversion is money well spent. More often than not, when an organization is left to its own devices without any outside guidance in the installation process, estimated costs are overrun, and timetables are not met. Inside personnel are most often too close to the issues to see problems before they arise. If nothing else, a consultant brings a fresh pair of eyes to the scene and fresh ideas to the table, allowing the staff to focus on their own jobs and implementation of the new technology. Consultants can provide staff the guidance necessary to make the transition smooth. They can also work with outside contractors if necessary, freeing internal personnel to deal with the day-to-day issues that arise during conversions. Additionally, consultants can be available for discussions about timetables, phases of implementation, costs, and processes involved, and for meetings with members of the board or donors to answer questions as necessary. Streamlining the process, giving the consultant the opportunity to affect the outcome, and setting up a hierarchy of command for the conversion will provide the tools necessary to make this very disruptive process run smoothly, and also will save the organization time and money in the long run.

The committee-driven approach

We all understand that a technological overhaul in an organization raises new personnel issues and problems. Minimizing these newly created problems and making any computer transition as easy as possible is management's goal. One method which I have found that works very well is a committee-driven approach to the change.

One might think that an issue as volatile as computer change should never be turned over to a committee, on the grounds that committee management of such an issue would create more havoc than strategy. However, I have found this not to be the case. Employees I know who served or are currently serving on a computer committee for the most part have good feelings about their role and the purpose of the committee. They believe they are accomplishing a very justifiable task and assisting the process of implementation.

The concept of having a committee manage the implementation of a major project is not new. Management courses such as TQM (Total Quality Management) present the use of committees as a significant way of involving employees in the decision-making process, henceforth empowering them with a sense of ownership of ideas and plans. This is a very critical part of helping a company deal with the fears that can arise during change, especially with something as disruptive as an overhaul of a computer system.

A committee of this nature should be composed of employees from all divisions, and represent all levels. Including a broad base in the decision process indicates clearly to employees that the organization recognizes their importance. Comprehensive inclusion also helps the organization most efficiently ascertain its needs. In addition, a member of the executive management team should sit on the committee. This person essentially acts as a sponsor, not only providing credibility to the team, but also having a voice about the work of the committee in executive-level meetings. This person need not serve as chair of the committee—it is enough to take the recommendations of the committee back to the executive director or president as decisions are made.

Public relations

It is important that through the process of a computer overhaul, the positive benefits of the change are made very clear to the staff and continuously reinforced. Too often, negative comments regarding any change become the rallying cry for those who are not comfortable with the prospect of adapting to a new system. Without an effort on the part of the organization to thwart this negative press, these ideas will take root and discourage the staff.

An organization should engage in a positive public relations campaign designed to convey (both internally and externally) the understanding that the computer change is necessary and cost-effective, and will enhance the work experience for everyone involved.

Conclusion

As we approach the twenty-first century, the skillful use of technology will become more and more a part of our workplace environments. Sophisticated development offices will be managing thousands of donors and data records. Those of us in this fundraising profession must remain aware of the latest technology in order to do our jobs effectively.

I hope I have provided some insights into the fears and issues facing those in the midst of technological change—which is really all of us. I think it is important for us to remember that change is inevitable. Or, as Richard Hooker so aptly said, "Change is not made without inconvenience, even from worse to better" (*Oxford Dictionary of Quotations*, 1966, p. 254).

Reference

Oxford Dictionary of Quotations. (2nd ed.) London: Oxford University Press, 1966.

PAUL J. MATIJEVIC *is currently donor services manager for the Chicago Symphony. Over the past eight years, he has worked for several nonprofit organizations in the Chicago area as director of development, corporate and foundation specialist, consultant, and software trainer.*

*Opera/Columbus, a small nonprofit organization,
successfully installed and adapted to a new computer system. This experience, described here, may
help others make the same transition.*

2

The implementation of a new system

Michael O. Ranney

THE ON-RAMP to the Information Superhighway doesn't have a fast
lane. As you move into cyberspace, the reality is that a step-by-
step process to select the right software and hardware will help to
avoid frustration and errors in judgment. In the case of Opera/
Columbus, this slow, thoughtful process was influenced by the
Opera's management team philosophy, the budget constraints
faced by most nonprofits, and the staff's competence and comfort
with computer technology. These are common circumstances for
the vast majority of nonprofits.

The setting

Opera/Columbus is not unique. It is a small nonprofit organization
with a staff of ten. Its budget is $1,500,000 to $1,700,000. In the
period I am describing, Opera staff was not particularly confident
about dealing with the technology it had in place, let alone dis-
cussing a more advanced system.

The Opera's computer system (if it can be called that) consisted
of six independent PCs, already well used before they were donated

NEW DIRECTIONS FOR PHILANTHROPIC FUNDRAISING, NO. 11, SPRING 1996 © JOSSEY-BASS PUBLISHERS

to the Opera in the early 1980s. Most of the PCs were bogged down, storing years of old correspondence and outdated databases. These machines, with memory stretched to near capacity, operated very slowly. Current staff just continued to add to the stored data and files, uncertain about breaking the habit of keeping everything.

No one remembered where most of the software had come from. There were all kinds of software discs but few manuals. In an office made up of the technologically challenged, most software sat on storage shelves. No one realized that it was inappropriate (not to mention illegal) to have the same copy of a program installed on each of the six PCs. The Opera's one copy of WordStar was the only consistent means we had to communicate with each other and the outside world. Few of the software packages lining the office shelves were actually licensed to the Opera.

An old laser printer produced letter-quality correspondence and materials. It was actually a good and reliable printer, although it was also well used before a local corporation donated it to the Opera. A second printer donated by a friend of the Opera lasted about six months before it quit working.

In a nonprofit arts environment where subscription data and contribution data were kept separately, the stage was set for an ongoing debate about how to reach our best donor prospects. It would be akin to a university development office not having access to alumni records or a hospital development department not knowing how to reach doctors or former patients. That debate fueled a general discussion about the inadequacy of our system.

A first taste of success

The first improvement in the system came as a new business manager sought to improve financial record keeping, while at the same time board members were expressing concerns about the accuracy of financial data. The software selected at that time still serves the Opera's needs—several upgrades later—for historic fiscal analysis, current income and expense data by line item, and future-year projections to correspond with the five-year business plan cycle used by the Opera.

Since it clearly demonstrated what was possible, the success of this software switch by the business office fueled further debate among staff members. There were a number of common concerns and needs, but as many, if not more, separate issues. There was a general concern about what controls could be placed on data to protect confidential information and limit access on a need-to-know basis. Discussions also dealt with the format of records and with what data needed to be kept. The ease of using records to produce letters or select data fields for analysis in reports for Opera decision makers were all raised as important issues.

A unique resource

A unique resource exists in Columbus, Ohio. CompuServe and the Columbus Foundation have funded a central computer system that many nonprofits use. Columbus Information Via Computer (CIVIC) offers a community calendar helpful for event planners; a membership database with fields tailored to each organization's unique needs; a contribution database to track giving in ways that meet each organization's requirements; a solicitation database that helps manage and track development campaign assignments, activity, and results; and an accounting database. CIVIC is located in the heart of downtown at Columbus' Center of Science of Industry. PCs and printers are available at that location for on-site work, and CIVIC may also be accessed by modem from remote locations. The security of each organization's records is carefully protected so that only authorized individuals may access data.

In the mid 1980s, the Opera's development department transferred its records from its internal database to CIVIC. There were several reasons for this transfer. Historic contribution records and the addition of prospect data to support campaign work had resulted in the accumulation of data beyond the capability of the Opera's database software. Planning multiple campaigns also necessitated research that produced even more data on individuals, corporations, and foundations. While the board enjoyed more useful reports from the business office, decision makers began to realize that better reporting could help in other areas.

Development office data files were somewhat improved by annual updates through CIVIC that coded current-year subscribers already in the development database and added as prospects those who were not in the development system. However, the process remained cumbersome, requiring significant manual checking and coding that often resulted in the creation of duplicate records.

At the same time, the marketing department and box office tested a number of software options for ticketing and record keeping. Unfortunately, the price for almost all these packages was prohibitive. In addition, most of the programs were strong for box office data but inadequate for contribution data. At the same time, upgrades in CIVIC and the success of the local ballet, symphony, and other arts organizations in keeping box office data in CIVIC attracted action.

Assembling an advisory group

Since staff felt they lacked the knowledge and expertise to make informed decisions about software and hardware needs, an effort was made to find friends of the Opera who could be consulted. A computer advisory group was assembled. It included six individuals from major local corporations who worked in the computer field.

An analysis was done of internal and external communication patterns and data needs. Flow charts were developed to show what information was needed and where it was needed. Graphic analysis of the patterns helped tremendously as we looked to meet current and future needs. This analysis helped to identify which staff members needed to have their own computers immediately as well as the staff members for whom shared computer time would be an adequate near-term solution.

The Computer Advisory Council helped staff develop several detailed solutions, including cost estimates, for the Opera's various computing needs. Proposed solutions ranged in complexity from stand-alone PCs to a fully networked Novell system. However, budget constraints forced the Opera to pursue and implement simpler solutions for at least the short term. These included deleting obsolete files on existing PCs, expanding memory on one PC, obtaining legal copies of the software currently in use, initiating some desktop publishing with the purchase of a copy of PageMaker, and creating an opportunity for key staff to get training in the computer software. Perhaps the most important step was the software training that the Opera was able to obtain from its corporate supporters. The training included several staff members who had not used computers before. In the end all staff members became more comfortable with basic word processing and spreadsheet software, thus greatly increasing the efficiency of the office.

At the same time, a technical assistance grant from the Ohio Arts Council enabled the Opera to evaluate its database in CIVIC, modify fields to accommodate box office and marketing record keeping needs, and consolidate box office and development records in the CIVIC system. Standards for data entry were created through technical assistance to help reduce the likelihood of duplicate entries and to create a consistent style for the Opera's records.

Removing obsolete databases and files from existing PCs made a difference in the speed of data processing. Staff became more knowledgeable about the impact of saving files and more discerning in selecting files to be retained. Removing the box office database freed up a significant amount of memory for desktop publishing and other functions.

Plans for implementing WordPerfect as the standard internal word processing software continued to meet with some resistance. Timing was the principal concern. We could not convert the office while we were in production because it would be too difficult to complete the work that was needed at that time and learn to use new software. We couldn't do it just before production for the same reason. When could we do it? "Let's wait a while," most people argued.

It was at about this time that the Opera moved into new office space. Instead of being crammed into small quarters, staff were now spread out in a two-story building. In anticipation of eventually doing something about our computer system, members of the Advisory Council suggested that when the new building was gutted and rewired, it should be equipped to handle more sophisticated computer networking. This work was done at a very modest additional cost and proved to be a key factor as we proceeded toward getting a new system up and running.

Strategic planning sessions were begun to create a new business plan for the Opera. There was reason for a more optimistic attitude. Ticket sales were growing. The operating campaign total was growing. Debt was being reduced. There was more energy and excitement around the Opera.

The strategic plan called for a four-year process to purchase new computer hardware and software; it would ultimately lead to a networked system with everyone having the same software. The plan called for the first phase to be the software and PCs for the development department. Thus the development department became the focal point for planning the new office system. The software and hardware decision made in the development department's phase of the project would guide the way for the rest of the project. Members of the Computer Advisory Council were consulted to help develop specifications for the system.

Defining software needs

The first step in this process was to define the software needs for development and the other areas of the office. The software decisions had to be made first because these needs defined many of the other dynamics of the system. For example, both hardware and staff training needs were determined by the software requirements.

Again the Computer Advisory Council was helpful. They arranged several demonstrations and software trials for the staff. We determined that we needed several types of software, including word processing, spreadsheet, database, presentation graphic package, schedule, internal e-mail, and software to support additional graphic work and scanning capability.

Making these determinations involved meetings among the staff and extensive discussions of various options, capabilities, and needs. The presence of outside experts and their opinions and logical explanations for recommended choices helped ease concerns and created a sense of comfort that we were heading in the right direction.

Defining hardware needs

Armed with the list of software choices, we requested bids from three hardware suppliers. The office configurations were discussed and data management flow charts were shared if requested. A vendor recommended by a member of the advisory council was the most impressive. This firm took the time to make several on-site visits, reviewing flow charts, talking with several staff, attending a staff meeting to ask and answer questions, and presenting a detailed bid that looked at two types of networks. This supplier recommended a Windows for Workgroups system, a network they had recently installed in an office similar to our own.

Finding training resources

At the same time, staff negotiated training in the use of all the different kinds of software to be used by the Opera. We located a local temporary employment agency willing to exchange computer training for an advertisement in the Opera's performance program. This generous offer further raised the level of staff interest in the implementation of the system and even brought about discussions of whether or not we could implement the entire system more quickly than called for in the business plan.

With training available for all staff, a major barrier to implementation of the system had been overcome. At the same time, more of the existing PCs began to have severe problems and several seemed ready for retirement.

Implementation

As we analyzed the bids, several points became clear:

- Implementing a system over a period of years meant that just when the system was complete, the components purchased initially would be ready for replacement. The Opera might not ever feel the full advantages of a complete new system, since parts would continually be added or changed. And by the time the full system was in place, it might well be inadequate for the Opera's needs.
- Existing PCs might not make it through the period planned for implementation.
- The goals regarding consistent and professional-looking correspondence would be met over time, rather than immediately. Some departments would be producing relatively poor quality correspondence and materials for years to come, reflecting badly on the Opera's image.
- Bids showing costs for the Windows for Workgroups system with ten PCs were lower than anticipated, and software and training costs had been reduced to well below budgeted levels. Opera/Columbus has a significant educational component included in its mission, so we were able to qualify for educational rates on software resulting in significant savings.
- Financing an immediate purchase of the entire system with pay-

ments spread over several years was still less expensive than the business plan had anticipated. All in all, the impact of immediate implementation would ultimately be greater efficiency and consistency in the professional appearance of correspondence and materials. As staff gained experience with the desktop publishing capabilities of the system, newsletters and other materials could be produced in-house at a savings.

The opera configuration

In the Windows for Workgroups configuration a hub connects all PCs with one PC acting as the file server. All PCs operate independently and have their own software installed. Windows for Workgroups includes a personal scheduler, internal e-mail, calculator, and other useful functions. The file server is used as the data storage location for corporate files. Individual PCs are used to store departmental data. File backup of all PCs is run though the file server. Through the file server hub connection, two printers (one upstairs and one downstairs) were able to efficiently serve the ten people on staff. Cost estimates included a scanner to facilitate desktop publishing and a high-speed dot matrix printer that would be shared throughout the system but used primarily with the business office for generating financial statements. Four PCs included fax modems, which others can access to send and receive faxes, or connect to CIVIC or the Internet. The system has capability for growth to incorporate additional PCs if needed. Software allows off-site access to the system via modem.

The day the system was installed was filled with excitement and anticipation. That day turned out to be several days. The process was rather complex as computers were connected into new wiring systems. We now knew how fortunate it was that a networked system had been anticipated at the time that the new wiring was installed. The supplier trained me in the installation of the software and I spent the next few evenings installing each of the programs.

Troubleshooting

Then the fun began. As the lead person on this project, I was the point of contact between staff and the vendor from whom we were purchasing the system. It was my job to ascertain what problems we could solve internally and what issues needed the attention of our vendor, and the vendor began training me on various aspects of the system. As time passed, more and more of the questions dealt with software issues: "How do I do this?" rather than with equipment problems. Referring people back to the software manuals only increased their frustration, so the development department (that is, my associate and I) made an effort to find answers to their questions.

Substantive hardware issues were referred to the vendor. It was with these that we knew that the time taken to investigate the question of service after installation had been worthwhile. The vendor was always willing to investigate problems, try solutions, and work to pinpoint the causes of the problems, gradually ruling out possibilities and striving to find answers. Countless hours were spent on troubleshooting issues as they came up, particularly difficulties relating to access to CIVIC, but others as well. Faulty PCs were replaced. A new hub was installed when the original failed. Gradually all components were working well and frustration subsided.

At the same time, staff began training in the software we had purchased and moved quickly through the self-paced training modules that were donated to us. The number of software questions subsided as everyone became more comfortable and knowledgeable about how things worked.

After a period of significantly lower productivity and efficiency, things began to work as we had expected. There were efficiencies with the new system. And internal and external communications were greatly improved. Reports and materials generated through the new system were of much better quality than anything we had been able to produce before.

Conclusion

So, five years after we began talking about a new computer system, we have one that is fulfilling our needs very well and is equipped with room to grow. We still have much to learn about the capabilities of the new system and as we do so we will be able to maximize its impact on our operations.

Our process for selecting the new system served us well and is worth summarizing here:

1. Internal and external analysis of the flow of communications and data needs
2. Evaluation of staff readiness for the system
3. Formation of an advisory group of people with computer experience
4. Working to maximize use of the existing system
5. Evaluating system options with input from staff and advisors
6. Selecting software that the new system will run
7. Contacting several potential suppliers about hardware options and costs
8. Selecting supplier with input from staff and advisors on the various options and with careful consideration given to record of support and service as provided by references
9. Planning for staff training

It can be tempting to move quickly through these decisions and skip steps. Consulting several individuals helped to keep us on track. I am not sure it would have occurred to us to plan for software before we decided on the hardware, but we were told by several people to decide on software first. I am not sure we would have given as much weight to post-installation service until our advisors stressed this. The issue of staff training would probably not have been given much consideration if had not been stressed by several of Opera's advisors. The most important advice we can offer is take your time and seek advice from a number of people with computer experience. As we managed a successful implementation and avoided costly mistakes, we were thankful for the slow pace, the caution, and the advice.

MICHAEL O. RANNEY, *CFRE, is currently director of development for Opera/Columbus, Columbus, Ohio. A graduate of Allegheny College, Meadville, Pennsylvania, Ranney attended the University of Manchester, England, and received his M.P.A. from the University of Pittsburgh Graduate School of Public and International Affairs.*

Changes in technology lead to changes in the management infrastructure required for successful fundraising.

3

Information and technology as management tools in today's development organization

Dale A. DiSanto

A MERE TWENTY YEARS AGO, we used Addressograph machines to manage development campaigns, and outstanding "card value" was a key factor in determining the potential for success. Over the past two decades, changes in technology have dramatically altered the way that fundraising is done and managed. Today, nearly all aspects of fundraising have been affected by new technologies.

Sophisticated development used to mean that an organization was conducting a capital campaign and hired a development consulting firm to conduct a feasibility study. This process included having the firm meet with top prospects, rate individuals of affluence, and determine their propensity to contribute to a campaign or program. A member of the consulting firm would then physically move to the site of the nonprofit organization and work as development counsel to manage volunteers and staff.

Today's sophisticated environment of development includes professional staff who not only conduct studies, but make the solicitations and manage campaigns that can be for hundreds of millions

NEW DIRECTIONS FOR PHILANTHROPIC FUNDRAISING, NO. 11, SPRING 1996 © JOSSEY-BASS PUBLISHERS

or even a billion dollars or more. They use advanced tools, such as Electronic Screening® of prospects, demographic and financial information concerning the net worth of individuals, and data about the value of real estate and stocks an individual owns.

When we hire a new major gifts development officer at the State University of New York, Buffalo, one of the first things we do during orientation is review the technology available to that officer. For starters, we provide a laptop with a fax modem for each development officer and provide background on the information resources available on our local area network, CD-ROMs, and databases.

Investing in people and technology

Just as fundraising organizations have grown and become more sophisticated, so has the complexity of the data management and technology they require to run efficiently. If your development office does not have current information and state-of-the-art technology, you are not on a level playing field with your competitors. Today it is not enough to have a top-flight staff; you must have the resources to know who your best prospects are and to understand their interests and affiliations. From a manager's perspective, you must know who is cultivating and soliciting the prospect, where in the cycle the solicitation process stands, and what the next steps are.

Many nonprofit organizations have learned that in order to obtain the positive benefits of philanthropic support, they must first invest adequate resources both in people and in technology. I do not know of any for-profit-enterprise where you can invest ten to twenty-five cents and can be assured of earning a dollar or more on your investment; however, in the development field such results are common. Accordingly, more organizations are committing substantial financial resources to achieve these significant returns on their investments.

In *Analyzing the Cost Effectiveness of Fund Raising*, a New Directions for Institutional Advancement publication, John Leslie (1979, pp. 68–69) points out a number of issues that today's development manager needs to consider. In this book, the variations in fundraising potential among colleges and universities are addressed. Leslie admits that spending too much time and money in determining gift potential is probably not the most practical use of hard-to-come-by dollars. However, he points out that money wisely invested on information systems will pay off handsomely in the assessment of potential. As we become more experienced at investing in our development programs, development will become more of a science and less of the art it presently is.

Recently, I met with Bruce Freeman, retired chairman of Marts & Lundy, one of the nation's largest and most experienced fundraising consulting firms. We discussed setting goals. In our conversation, Freeman confirmed that there is no exact science to goal setting. No consultant or computer can tell a development officer exactly how much can be raised. He said, "There are a number of people using computer-generated systems to establish goals. However, these computerized comparisons do not take into consideration the nature of the institution or the nuances of that institution." The best we can do to establish goals is to make logical estimates, using past giving history, current feasibility studies, and common sense. Goal setting is one task that should always be done by humans. While computers are vital tools, they will never be able to understand what motivates a donor to make a major commitment to a nonprofit organization.

In the past several years, many development programs, especially in higher education, have become large and sophisticated operations, with the hierarchies, resources, and managerial expertise of small or midsize corporations. Several institutions of higher education have conducted capital campaigns with goals that exceeded one billion dollars.

Where there are organizations pursuing campaigns with goals that are the same size as the gross income of Fortune 500 companies, I can assure you that there are adequate resources invested in people and in technology and that there are dedicated people that manage both the information resources as well as the people that utilize them.

Harvard University employs more than 250 people who are associated with their development operation. The Wharton School of

Business at the University of Pennsylvania employs over 50 individuals who work in advancement and development. At Ohio State University there are about 120 people who work in the Development and Alumni Relations Office. The point here is that institutions are investing significant resources in staff and in budgets and are providing their development offices with the state-of-the-art tools to do their jobs.

The fundraising cycle

All good development starts with research. The next process is the development of a strategy, then cultivation, solicitation, and stewardship—and then the process starts over again. Today there are numerous tools available to inform development officers about the prospects from whom they are seeking funds. In addition to the information available about prospects, such as the value of their homes or the stocks they may own, firms now do Electronic Screening® of the information on entire databases. This information takes into consideration a variety of demographic factors such as the value of real estate in the area where the prospect lives and similar secondary indications of the prospect's general prosperity.

The more up-front research an organization does, the better off it will be in establishing realistic goals, developing effective solicitation strategies, raising major gifts, and successfully completing campaigns.

Prospect tracking systems

In a large organization, coordination of prospect management becomes a critical factor. A development manager cannot afford to have several colleges, schools, deans, or development officers competing with each other and approaching the same prospects for different projects. Information technology becomes critical in this sort of coordination.

This past year at Buffalo, we knew that we were planning a major computer conversion from an antiquated system into a comprehensive and sophisticated development system called BSR Advance. With approximately 110,000 alumni, we needed a database that could handle a lot of records, and also one that would be user friendly and easy to manage. It was important for management to outline and define the needs that the new system should support. Accordingly, we had (and have) a number of software and computer professionals working with our development staff in defining how the software would serve as a management tool for our organization. With a total investment of approximately $500,000, it was important that the system provide the information that our management staff and development officers need to do their jobs.

We also knew, however, that in the meantime it was imperative that we do prospect management and tracking of major donor prospects. Development does not stop just because we are working on an upgrade and a major conversion. Accordingly, we obtained a copy of a relational database called Paradox for Windows, which anyone can buy and configure to suit specific needs. We used Paradox to design our own prospect tracking management tool, knowing all the while that it was just a temporary fix until our new client-server software was installed.

A prospect tracking system is one of the most important tools a development office can have. It helps prioritize prospects and track who is cultivating and soliciting them. And in so doing, a tracking system also prevents the conflict of several officers soliciting the same prospects. In fundraising, as in any business, it is very important that all aspects of management are aware of the priority initiatives each is working toward.

With this idea of shared information in mind, our new system at Buffalo will be accessed through a local area network managed by our central development office. We are also in the process of placing our prospect tracking system on CD-ROM, so our development staff can use this system from several sites on campus. Our current plans include keeping several CD-ROMs up to date. We are hopeful that with everyone having the capability to retrieve and update information on the same database, we will indeed have our hands synchronized—as well as outstretched!

In addition, our planned giving staff has seen to it that their software, PG Calc, is available to all users on our network. PG Calc's software, Planned Giving Manager® is an excellent tool for running calculations such as the payments of gift annuities and charitable remainder trusts.

At Penn State University, the executive director of development, Robert N. Groves, regularly meets with deans and development staff to review and monitor their progress. As a part of managing the programs at Penn State, he has available to him information on several key development factors, such as listings of all prospects anyone on the staff is visiting, where prospects are located, the status of major donor prospects, and the financial results that each officer is achieving. Other factors regularly reviewed include the status of each college or unit in relation to its goals and next steps major gifts officers will take in attempts to complete gifts. All of this coordination points out the vast requirements that today's development offices have for statistics and research.

David Dunlop, director of capital projects at Cornell University, related how Cornell utilizes prospect tracking (Dunlop and Ryan, 1990). He said, "A good tracking system is your basic tool to manage, coordinate, communicate and stimulate major fund-raising activity. It identifies who you're dealing with—not only prospects, but also primes, secondaries and staff managers. It records your targets, what you hope for the next gift, what you want it for, and how to plan your work toward it. Most important, it tells how your plans fit in with recent history. It records previous plans and events so you can see why you did or didn't make certain moves."

Management and development

Recently, *Business Week* featured a cover story with the headline: "The Horizontal Corporation. Hierarchy is dying. In the new corporate model, you manage across—not up and down. Here's How" (Byrne, 1993). The lesson of this article is that workers now organize around process—not task—and utilize teams to manage everything. I believe that this model will become more predominant, not only for corporations, but also for the nonprofit sector. The utilization of technology by sophisticated managers will help foster organizations that are less hierarchical and more flat in the future. Technology has empowered managers to not only do their jobs better, but to work more effectively with clients (donors) and collaborate with colleagues. Peter Drucker, the well-known author of several books on management, recently decided to focus his attention on the nonprofit or the third sector. In his book *The New Realities* (1989), Drucker predicted—before re-engineering or corporate managerial flattening became popular—that in twenty years the typical large organization will have half the levels of management of its counterpart of the day. Drucker also predicted that computer technology will change the way organizations run and are managed. He said, "The information-based organization requires self-discipline and an emphasis on individual responsibility for relationships and for communications" (pp. 207–208).

Need for people who are computer literate

In years gone by, development staff could relegate the information side of the business to the management information systems department. Today's development officer needs to understand how to operate a computer, including software and modems, and how to communicate through electronic mail or the Internet. At Buffalo, all our development staff need to understand our word processing and spreadsheet software, as well as our prospect tracking system. In addition, development staff need to understand the programs that run development operations and finances. In today's development organization, the research staff are required to access a number of publications and resources in order to do an effective job. At our organization, we use on-line services provided through firms such as CDA Investnet, CompuServe, Lexis-Nexis, the Foundation Center, and Standard & Poor's, among others.

Commitment to continued education

In addition to having the tools available for staff to use, larger development offices provide staff training on new machines, systems, and software. Being a major university, Buffalo already has a great deal of computer knowledge readily available to our staff. In addition, we have staff members dedicated to computing for development; their responsibilities include not only maintenance of systems but also the training of staff. Recently, two vendors made presentations to all of our officers to explain how to best access and use the software and consulting services we had purchased.

New expectations from donors

While development offices are becoming more sophisticated, so are donors. They expect that development staff provide deliverables on gifts, such as reports on scholarship funds, rates of return on gift annuities, and similar computerized information. Just as today's development staff have new tools, so do the donors and prospects they work with. While I have not as yet communicated with a donor through the Internet, my address is on my business card and I certainly expect that it will become a means of donor communications.

The right information for the right organization

As mentioned earlier, our organization decided to invest in new software and do a major conversion, combining all of our systems into one. Before we decided on a system, we looked at what other major universities were using and asked them about their experiences with the programs they purchased. We learned that many of the nation's largest development organizations were using one of three software packages.

While having this information made it easier to make a decision, we still did a thorough analysis of systems and selected the one that best fit our needs. Because our old system was known by many on the campus community to be antiquated, we invited all the deans and development staff from all the schools and major departments to participate in the process of reviewing and evaluating various systems.

Just because a computer system is complex does not mean it is the right one for an organization. While many organizations are working to secure the resources to purchase today's technology, each organization is different and has different computer and technology needs. The computer system that is good for a large organization like a major research university may not be the best one for a smaller nonprofit organization. A few years ago, I consulted with a nonprofit organization that employed approximately fifteen staff members in its development office. The organization had purchased the same computer system that universities like Harvard and Penn State employ, and the executive director confided that they do not use about 90 percent of the software they purchased. In addition, the organization spent about ten times as much money as they needed to spend on software. Obviously, resources were not used effectively. While the organization also probably felt that it was buying for the future, the software they purchased is already out of date, due to the new technology that is now available.

The proliferation of technology

CASE *Currents* recently published an article entitled "Bucking the System. Mad at Your Alumni/Development Software? Dreaming of What the Next Upgrade Will Do? Six Campus Professionals Sound Off" (Littlefield, 1995). One of the things I found interesting in this article is that the author—a senior consultant with Grenzebach,

Glier Development and Management Consulting—listed more than fifty companies that provide client/server systems for development use. In addition, the article listed ten vendors in the minicomputer and mainframe system business. The cost of the software that the client/server companies provide varies from $145 to $500,000. The average system sells in the range of $3,000 to $10,000. More important, the author points out that what may have cost $250,000 ten years ago may only cost a few thousand dollars today.

How long should implementation take?

For a large organization with a large number of records, a conversion generally should take from twelve to twenty-four months. Of course, there are many factors that affect this time frame. In addition, one should consider that technology is constantly changing. Last year's 486 computer may not be fast enough to run programs that require a pentium chip. In addition, with the advent of Windows, many programs both large and small are trying to be user-friendly; you may need to upgrade the program you just purchased in a few years.

The human factor

At any organization, the development staff must know who their prospects are and what their potential to give is; the staff must have the ability to determine each prospect's propensity to make major commitments. While information and technology are keys to assist in this process, we know that most people will not respond in a significant way to either a phone call or a direct mail piece. While we live in an era of sophisticated technology, major commitments are made as a result of development staff (along with organizational leadership and many times volunteers) soliciting prospects face to face. The computer on a staff member's desk cannot take the place of personal cultivation. Therefore, technology can and should be seen as a tool that assists an organization with its work.

While computers are vital tools, they will never be able to understand what motivates a donor to make a major commitment to a nonprofit organization.

Where is all of this going?

In "Asking for a Gift: Volunteers or Staff—Which is Best?" Abbie Von Schlegell and Barry McGannon (1990) discuss how the development profession has become more professional. They state that "90–95 percent of the work takes place before the ask itself." We are now in the age of the megacampaign. Those institutions that invest in the infrastructure to permit major gifts staff to do their jobs effectively will be the institutions that will be raising not millions of dollars in the future, but billions of dollars. Without the proper research, computers, and tools to conduct development programs effectively, institutions will falter and some will go the way of the dinosaur. The former football coach at Ohio State University, Woody Hayes, used to say, "Winning takes care of everything." Those institutions that invest both in people and in technology will be the winners in this era of multimillion dollar gifts and megacampaigns.

References

Byrne, J. "The Horizontal Corporation," *Business Week*, Dec. 20, 1993, pp. 76–77.

Drucker, P. F. *The New Realities.* New York: HarperCollins, 1989.

Dunlop, D., and Ryan, E. "Thirty Years of Fund Raising," CASE *Currents*, Nov./Dec. 1990, p. 34.

Leslie, J. W. *Analyzing the Cost Effectiveness of Fund Raising.* New Directions for Institutional Advancement, no. 3. San Francisco: Jossey-Bass, 1979.

Littlefield, J. "What's Where in Software: An Update," CASE *Currents*, May 1995, pp. 32–37.

Von Schlegell, A., and McGannon, J. B. "Asking for a Gift: Volunteers or Staff—Which Is Best?" Working paper from National Society of Fund Raising Executives' International Conference, Orlando, Fla., Mar. 1990.

DALE A. DISANTO *is executive director of major gifts and capital projects at the State University of New York, Buffalo. Previously, DiSanto served the United Way, Franklin University, Riverside Methodist Hospitals, and Ohio State University.*

*On-line technology can support the typical func-
tions of a fundraising office, but also poses some risks.
Here is a summary of the techniques, tools, and dangers of using telecommunications in this setting.*

4
─────────

Fundraising and the Information
Superhighway

Deborah Strauss

THE CONCEPT OF THE COMPUTER as an essential tool to improve the
inner workings of an organization is well established for anyone who
has worked in a fundraising office over the past decade. What isn't
so well established is the concept of the computer as an essential tool
for *external* communication. Yet using technology to ride the Information Superhighway holds important potential for fundraising
activities, and those who adopt it early will reap meaningful rewards.

The Superhighway and the Internet threaten to become fad topics—they are being covered extensively in the media, but little has
been written or presented about the specific application of these
new tools to development work. Therefore, this article discusses
the current possibilities for using newer technologies in the
fundraising setting and emphasizes the choices that are likely to
confront development professionals. The focus here is on on-line
tools using computers and telephone lines; while television and
radio broadcasting and cable casting and telephony are certainly
important aspects of the information transfer process and present

NEW DIRECTIONS FOR PHILANTHROPIC FUNDRAISING, NO. 11, SPRING 1996 © JOSSEY-BASS PUBLISHERS

policy and implementation issues of their own, they are not the topic of this chapter.

A few caveats: first, technology *per se* is not really my subject; rather, my concern is improving the efficiency of the work that fundraisers already do—and gaining that improvement at a reasonable cost. Technology is simply a tool to achieve that improvement. Therefore, the language here is English and not computerese, and there is no attempt to be comprehensive: readers are assumed to be computer users at basic levels but to have no expertise in telecommunications. Brief definitions will be interspersed; pointers to specific on-line sites will be found in the reference section at the end of the chapter. A telecommunications primer is offered as Section I; experienced users may want to skip to Section II.

Second, as this is written, usage of on-line services is at approximately 30 million worldwide and growing at the rate of 200,000 new users per month! Obviously, availability and costs change rapidly as the industry responds. What is not possible today because of technical limitations will be possible next month; connectivity and pricing information that is accurate today will soon be incorrect. Rather than deal in specifics in an environment full of moving targets, I'm emphasizing capabilities that are now or will soon be available at reasonable cost throughout North America, and I am emphasizing mainstream technologies, those that will probably be adopted by large numbers of users.

Section I: Telecommunications primer

In order to go on line, the minimum requirements are a computer (any kind, any vintage—although older and slower machines have limitations), and a telephone line that can be dedicated to this use when you are actually using the system. You must either have telecommunications software such as Procomm (which may have been bundled with your computer), or you may use a commercial service such as America Online or CompuServe, which provides the software. You must have a modem, which may be inside your computer. Modems are rated in bits (binary integers) per second, known as bps; faster is better. In early 1995, the slowest modem one might buy would be 9600 bps at $50 or so; 14.4 kbps (kilobits per second) modems costing between $100 and $150 would be typical; and an ideal choice would be a 28.8 bps v.34 modem costing $150 to $250, the fastest dial-up now available.

For a fundraising office wanting to make active and efficient use of telecommunications, the minimums will not be satisfactory. The computer should be Windows-compatible or Macintosh; the modem should be at least 14.4; the telephone lines should be arranged so that on-line usage does not restrict voice telephone usage; and the access provider should offer full Internet capability, special services related to your mission or circumstances, or both.

You must have an access provider. There are several options, and it is relatively easy to switch. Your initial decision about service providers is not a lifetime commitment. Options include:

• *Commercial services,* for instance, America Online, Compu-Serve, or Prodigy, costing about $10 per month for a basic usage package—five hours per month. Commercial services all provide electronic mail to any e-mail user (not just their own subscribers). They each offer access to their own package of services (such as libraries of periodicals, databases, and user forums) that vary from one provider to another. Commercial services provide varying degrees of access to the Internet.

• *Direct Internet providers,* companies that provide you with a local access number who generally charge a flat fee ($25 per month, for example) for an ample allotment of service—say, one hundred hours per month. These companies do not typically have the extra services found on the commercial services. Users affiliated with universities generally have this type of access (at no fee to the user) via their institutions.

• *Nonprofit providers,* for instance, HandsNet, Institute for Global Communications (IGC), and ArtsWire, aimed specifically at nonprofits. HandsNet is oriented to social service organizations across the country, maintaining databases and forums specific to the topic. IGC maintains EcoNet and PeaceNet, with concentrations of services on the environment and conflict resolution, respectively. ArtsWire serves arts organizations nationwide. While all providers offer e-mail to the on-line universe, there may be limitations on other Internet usage.

Another requirement is training, delivered either in short courses or in print materials. While the commercial services generally provide self-starting discs and on-screen instructions, most users find that external training resources minimize frustration and maximize their grasp of the various options. A source of on-site or telephone troubleshooting should also be arranged; training courses and manuals, comprehensive as they may be, don't always overcome all the obstacles to getting new users hooked up and signed on.

Section II: Why go on line?

Why should your organization venture onto the Information Superhighway and what benefits and risks should be expected? Without preamble, I want to begin with the obvious question—can you raise money on line? Is cyberspace the source of a new donation stream for your organization?

I've learned that it's dangerous to say "It doesn't work" when new or unusual fundraising methods are under discussion, because someone on the committee can always come up with an instance when it did work. So I'll never say *never.* Efforts *are* underway to raise money on line, some originated by organizations with a nonprofit mission, others originated by for-profit enterprises promoting services claiming to help you get your message out and raise dollars via telecommunications. Some of the nonprofit efforts are collaborative, involving several related organizations operating under a single banner. These efforts are being publicized (in print and on the Net) but the results are so far either disappointing or unspecified. Obviously, someone could be having great success in raising money on the Internet and not telling the rest of us, but except for that possibility, and for the likelihood that organizations on line primarily for other purposes may be receiving some by-product donations, direct solicitation is not the reason to make the superhighway journey at this time. There are several reasons:

• Consumers are reluctant to put credit card data on line for any sort of transaction. There is great interest in retail business in reaching consumers through this medium, and solutions to the credit card problem are at hand because of immense pressure to facilitate transactions, but even as the technical problems are solved, user confidence in the security of this interaction will take time to develop.

• One alternative response vehicle is a transient image of a form on a screen, which the user downloads, prints, and mails back in an envelope with a check. With the onus of effort placed on the respondent, returns are not likely to be impressive. Another method is providing an 800 number so the user can make a telephone call to initiate a credit card transaction or request contribution materials, but this process too demands initiative and a separate step by the prospective donor.

• Many users pay for on-line service on a timed basis and they will not visit sites that do not promise gratification of some identified need of their own; spending money only to be asked for money goes against basic human nature. Further, many popular areas of the Internet forbid direct solicitation for sales or contributions.

With that said, there remain many compelling reasons for implementing on-line activities in the typical development offices—the main ones being communications and research. *Communications* is here defined very broadly—it includes interaction with:

• Board members, committee members, and key volunteers
• Constituents, donors, and prospective donors
• Colleagues outside your organization
• The media and funders
• The general public

Research is defined as information gathering in regard to funding sources:

- Government grant programs
- Foundation guidelines, priorities, and grants listings
- Corporate giving programs and on business data related to philanthropy
- Individual prospects
- Development of funded programs, for example, community needs assessment data, scholarly work, and model programs

How can telecommunications add value to each type of communication? Which telecommunications tools—electronic mail, list servers, newsgroups, World Wide Web pages, Gopher—are most useful for which activities? Since certain telecommunications tools have broad applicability across the spectrum of audiences addressed by development offices while others are related to a particular function, I'll introduce each tool as we discuss the function with which it is most often associated.

Communication—electronic mail

The most commonly used telecommunications tool is electronic mail; many entities have e-mail linking offices within a building or within an institution and are therefore familiar with its benefits. But the Information Superhighway takes e-mail outside your walls and around the world. Think of the time we all spend on the routine communications tasks of everyday organizational life—setting up meetings, passing on bits of news, inquiring about a deadline, clarifying an agenda item, getting approval for documents or plans, and so on. Development offices, which place a high value on involving many external individuals in meetings, decisions, campaigns, and events, can make excellent use of electronic mail in all these activities.

Electronic mail is the one application that is common across all telecommunications services; every user has an e-mail address and all the sender needs to know is the recipient's address and that he or she checks the mailbox regularly. Messages can be sent to a single individual or to preselected groups of individuals—say the membership of a particular committee—each of whom receives a private message. And once a group address is keyed into one's electronic address book, it takes no more time to reach a group of people than to reach one individual. A mailed meeting announcement for eight people costs 32¢ apiece plus the time for printing labels and stuffing envelopes; a fax for each, even if your machine is programmed for the group, still carries the cost of eight phone calls—local or long distance as the case may be.

The advantages of e-mail for day in, day out communication needs are several. E-mail avoids telephone tag, misunderstood messages on crumpled pink slips, truncated or garbled messages on telephone tapes, and trips to the fax machine. It allows for time shifting—that is, it allows you to send and receive information at any convenient time or from work or home without regard to business hours or the whereabouts of the other party. It decreases the number of telephone interruptions each day, it saves paper, postage, express mail, and messenger costs because of all the memos that do not have to be printed and delivered. Complete documents can be circulated for input and approval, with recipients making additions or deletions right on the screen and returning the document to the sender within minutes.

While e-mail directories analogous to phone books are just beginning to be developed, there are ways to locate individual addresses under certain circumstances; most often, however, individuals exchange e-mail addresses personally or list them on business cards. As organizations publish their own addresses and begin to receive e-mail, staff should capture the addresses of their correspondents to make sure the connection is maintained.

Development officers, taught to value personal relationships and face-to-face communication with key individuals, may wonder whether e-mail will impede these relationships. The fact that e-mail generally reduces (but does not eliminate) the need for meetings, visits, and telephone conversations to get organizational tasks accomplished may engender fear that the cultivation usually woven into these activities may be lessened if the computer becomes the medium of routine exchange.

I argue that e-mail is not an impersonal medium. For many users, it is easier than picking up the phone or formally putting thoughts on paper, and for these people, it encourages communication. People who will not return phone calls or write to their class agents will initiate e-mail. Further, development staff themselves may find it easier to maintain a high level of individualized communication with a large number of constituents using this tool. One does develop a personality on line. By being easy and inexpensive and spontaneous, e-mail can increase the frequency of communication. Finally, constituents who use e-mail regularly like the medium and react with impatience when they are unable to use it in appropriate situations.

One of the typical applications for e-mail in a development situation is as a means of responding to constituents, volunteers, or donors, especially when two-way communication is desirable. College and university alumni magazines frequently publish e-mail addresses to elicit letters to the editor and alumni news. Organizations that mobilize cadres of volunteers to participate in major environmental or building projects can do much of the contact and follow-up work on line. And orchestrating "athons" becomes much easier when e-mail is one of the tools.

The quality of development committee and special event planning meetings can be improved with the use of e-mail. Agendas can be developed and amended or approved by several individuals without a single phone call. Participants can be educated about key issues before the meeting; they can be alerted politely but repeatedly about their assignments and deadlines, and consensus building can begin before the meeting takes place.

One caveat: no matter how enthusiastic you or *some* of your constituents are about using e-mail for organizational tasks, there will be a period of time when dual communication systems must be maintained or you risk losing the involvement of those who do not have access to telecommunications or who choose not to use it. The length of this time period will vary according to your population, and some individuals who are important to your organization will never adapt. Too much enthusiasm about technology may deflect interest from your cause or lead to withdrawal on the part of people who feel that they can't be in the inner circle if they aren't on line. At the same time, don't be misled by stereotypes into incorrect assumptions about what types of people are and are not hooked up. While the preponderance of on-line users are younger college-educated males, a surprising number of middle-aged women with children away at college have found their way to their offspring's electronic mail boxes, and retired individuals hang around on senior networks. There are other people who have put off telecommunications because they had no specific purpose in going on line, but participation in your organization's work may be the impetus they need.

To encourage but not mandate on-line use, you may want to identify a particular commercial on-line service or local Internet provider (if your constituents are located in one geographic area) and offer demo disks, discounted accounts arranged with the provider, and simple training sheets about reaching you on that system. While your fundraising entity is not in business to support any particular system, your leadership in identifying a service can help potential users over the hump of making the decision. Any of these efforts, however, should be done from the perspective of technology being a means and not an end.

E-mail also has relevance in the many other kinds of communication that make up our business lives. Essentially, any kind of information that might be exchanged in a brief phone call or fax can be transferred to e-mail, whether it is setting up the program for the next meeting of fundraisers in your city, asking for advice from a mentor, arranging for a support letter from an allied organization, or in the case of some forward-looking foundations, seeking guidance on some aspect of a proposal.

Communication—list servers and newsgroups
So far, we've been talking about only one telecommunications tool—e-mail—which involves one-to-one communication and

mimics the telephone, fax, and paper mail systems with which we are all familiar. There are several other tools that provide forms of communication that are truly new—they don't mimic anything and force a real change in our thinking about communication. These tools—list servers, usenet newsgroups, and World Wide Web pages—already have many development office applications, and new possibilities continue to emerge.

List servers and newsgroups are closely related in function and sometimes duplicate one another; the differences have to do with the fact that not all systems have the same technological capabilities, and with personal preference. Newsgroups provide a central repository of messages on a specific topic and require additional software; list servers deliver messages directly to an e-mail address and thus are available even to users who do not have other Internet access. Both allow for "many-to-many" communication in the form of exchanges of messages among individuals anywhere in the world who have subscribed to the list server or newsgroup because of an interest in the topic. There are more than eight thousand newsgroups by topic, some very serious and some entirely frivolous. There are several list servers and newsgroups for fundraisers, nearly all from the United States and Canada, including one group for prospect researchers, another primarily for development staff in higher education, and another for general nonprofit management questions.

Using these tools, individuals can find out how things are done in other institutions (How does your database deal with alumnae who change their names when they marry?), ask for advice for specific situations (My campaign chairman wants me to fax prospect information, but I don't trust his office staff to keep the information confidential), develop strategy (When is it appropriate to send multiple proposals for the same project?), discuss ethics (Should we pay grant writers on commission?), build networks (Let's all get together at the next NSFRE or CASE conference), learn about new government funding initiatives (The latest guidelines for the Department of Commerce Telecommunications Infrastructure grants were issued today—they are available at the following on-line address), or they can be used simply to stay abreast of the concerns of fundraisers.

The idea of exchanging information with hundreds or even thousands of people, yet doing it informally, frequently, and on an individualized basis, is radical. On the same day, one can be a questioner or an expert; one can enter a fray or watch quietly from the sidelines; one can develop an on-line personality or reputation for expertise on a specific topic or one can remain entirely anonymous. The user learns to phrase questions appropriately, to be skeptical because not everyone who offers an answer to a question is truly an expert, and to move to e-mail when an interchange is important only to two people, not the whole group.

Yet another use of these tools is for subject matter investigation as opposed to the functional topics mentioned above. Many of those eight thousand groups are on topics related to common nonprofit organizational missions such as specific health concerns, urban development, substance abuse, activism, environment, and so on. Topics such as education are broken down into a myriad subtopics (for instance, education.adult, education.home-school.christian, education.home-school.misc, education.language.english, education.learning-disability; the subtopic education.K-12 is further subdivided). For another example, newsgroups on the topic of AIDS include hiv.actup-actnow, hiv.aids.issues, hiv.alt-treatments, hiv.announce, hiv.planning, hiv.resources.addresses, to name a few. While most of these are for the general public rather than for practitioners or staff at service organizations, they offer news, commentary, debate, and questions, and provide a window into the minds of consumers concerned with a specific issue.

Communication—World Wide Web

While I'm skeptical about on-line fundraising, I am very enthusiastic about using the Internet for the broad variety of communication tasks carried on in nonprofit offices. While marketing general services, announcing events, recruiting volunteers, providing mission-specific information, countering misinformation, and publicizing your position on controversial topics may not directly generate funds, these functions certainly support your fundraising effort. The World Wide Web, an Internet tool with rich graphics, the possibilities of sound and animated images, and text linking powers, became generally available in 1994 and is currently generating a great deal of excitement because of its marketing and outreach capabilities.

The Web allows an organization to develop its own presentation, called a *page*. Pages are found according to addresses called Uniform Resource Locators (URLs), which are listed in directories, in organizational literature and presentations, and in linkages from related Web pages. A page can be thought of as an on-screen brochure; it typically has colorful graphics including an organizational logo and other pictures interspersed with text; it describes the organization and presents a series of choices so viewers click on their selections. Integrated in the text are links, denoted in color, that take the viewer to related information at other Web pages. Most Web pages include a direct e-mail link, making it almost effortless for the viewer to send e-mail to the sponsoring organization.

For instance, a Web page for a zoo would begin with general information about the zoo's collection, location, hours of operation, and so on. Viewers would click on choices such as special zoo events, baby animals, children's programs, volunteers needed, membership benefits and costs, publications for purchase, and ordering instructions. The baby-animals choice would certainly include pictures of the zoo's newborns—and perhaps small sound clips as well. Choices such as large mammals would include links that would take the viewer to the natural history museum and its collection of extinct mammals; the aquatic section might include a link to the local aquarium, and the children's programs section might include a link to a page for school teachers detailing citywide field trip possibilities. A Web page might include an option labeled "how to make a contribution to the zoo," but the real purpose of the Web page is general promotion of the organization and building attendance and interest in special programs.

Web pages carry some cost. They must be written in a special programming language, which is relatively easy to learn, and they should have graphics built in. Space on a server must be acquired, generally at a moderate monthly fee. Developing appropriate information options and information linkages takes some staff time, as does updating the page as programs change. However, compared to the costs of publishing and mailing brochures, or of buying media advertising, costs are very small and the audience reached this way is growing rapidly. The technology provides feedback on usage—for instance, the American Red Cross page (on a national basis), which included local program information, information about the latest disasters where the Red Cross is involved, volunteer recruitment and more, received 9,600 *hits*—that is, individual instances of people looking at the page—during its twelfth week of existence nationwide.

Research—Gopher and World Wide Web

Research relating to fundraising is a very important electronic activity although it is too soon to cancel your subscriptions to hard-copy research materials or eliminate trips to the library. For the purposes of this chapter, which focuses on the Internet, it is important to distinguish Internet information—usually contained in Gopher sites or the World Wide Web and available for no extra charge (although the user may be paying for access to the Internet)—from the data obtained via special services such as Dialog, Dow Jones News Retrieval, Disclosure, Lexis-Nexis, and the Foundation Center. These services use the Information Superhighway and are reached via computer, modem, and telephone lines, but are separate from the Internet and carry subscription and timed use charges. Many have special relevance for certain kinds of fundraising, such as individual prospect research on Dialog and current corporate profitability on Disclosure, and development staff with specific responsibilities will want to understand the relevance of these services for the work they do.

Gopher is a distributed document search and retrieval system. (While the World Wide Web involves a graphical user interface and allows for pictures and point-and-click access, Gopher is entirely text-based.) It provides a method for browsing through vast collections of information located in server machines anywhere in the world. The name comes from the mascot at the University of

Minnesota, the academic home of Gopher development and is also a play on the term go-fer. There are several Gophers with the word *grants* in their titles; most are maintained by universities and emphasize grant programs specific to higher education; others pertain to a certain scientific discipline. The Foundation Center in New York maintains a Gopher (although its searchable grants index is only available via Dialog, one of the fee-for-service inquiry systems). The federal government's Catalog of Federal Domestic Assistance is available via Gopher, and more important, nearly every arm of the government posts its own information—including grant availability—on the Internet, although there is variance in the amount of material available. The Department of Commerce Telecommunications Information Infrastructure Administration Program (TIIAP) is exemplary in posting full grant guidelines and ample information about last year's successful applicants; letters of intent for this program can be submitted electronically as well. Another resource for government funding information is Hands-Net, a subscription electronic network for nonprofits emphasizing social services. HandsNet repackages information about government funding in its areas of interest and regularly alerts subscribers about opportunities.

Free information about corporate grants is not yet compiled anywhere on the Internet in a searchable and consistent way; print directories remain the best tools for researching corporate giving opportunities. However, once you've focused on a few potential corporate funders, it is worth checking to see if they have World Wide Web pages publicizing their guidelines—a step that certain corporate funders are considering. Other corporate information relevant to donations (10-Ks, listings of plants and products, listings of individual board member holdings in proxy statements) is generally only available on Dialog or its competitors, as is individual who's-who type information about prominent executives. As corporate Web pages become more prevalent, this sort of business information is likely to become available via the Internet.

Regarding foundations, several (including the John D. and Catherine T. MacArthur Foundation and the Carnegie Corporation) have Web pages of their own at http://www.macfdn.org and www.carnegie.org, respectively. These pages typically display information about program interests, guidelines, and contact address books; MacArthur also posts grants listings. I would look for many more foundations to develop Web pages in the near term, but because there are differences of opinion in the foundation world about just how accessible each wishes to be, I am less confident that e-mail communication with program officers and electronic proposal submission will soon be widespread.

Some new services related to fundraising and requiring subscriptions have recently appeared on the Web and on commercial services. In certain localities such as Chicago and Kansas City, on-line research tools, specific to the area, are also available.

Section III: Risks of telecommunications usage

For someone considering introducing on-line usage to a development office, what are the management concerns? We already hear jokes about the boss key—the one that hides the game on the screen when the boss walks by. Just as there are risks in putting a telephone on a desk or a game anywhere in the computer system, wasted time and excessive costs billed to the organization are a risk of on-line work. Security issues and inappropriate references to your organization are other risks.

The manager should assume every new user will waste some time—that is, explore on-line areas that have no relation to your organization's work. But adults with a good work ethic are likely to waste no more time on line than they waste other ways, once they are familiar with the Internet's potential. Yes, they will use your system to send e-mail to a child away at college if they don't have a system at home, but this probably will cost you little or no cash and only a few minutes of staff time—this kind of usage is best thought of as equivalent to tolerable levels of personal phone time.

Inappropriate use of the organization's identity by staff (for instance, insulting another individual on line or making comments in an Internet area focusing on recreational sex) can be minimized by a written policy detailing permissible activities, supplemented by reminders that users are in some sense representing their organization when using an employer's account. Other concerns focus on the security of organizational data when networked machines are used for on-line work. There are dangers from viruses coming into your machines and from outsiders intruding into your data. However, viruses are usually found only in program files. It is impossible to hide a virus in a text file and difficult to hide one in an enclosed document, so surfing the Net does not transmit viruses. The risk is present only when files are downloaded, and the serious risk occurs only when program files are downloaded.

There are other dangers in moving into Internet marketing activities without full consideration of whether these electronic tools are truly integrated into the organization's overall marketing and mission. For instance, are the on-line materials fully consistent in design, tone, and content with other organization publications and outreach strategies? Is the organization ready to respond to an influx of inquiries requiring quick response and service? On-line communications hit immediately, unlike typical marketing campaigns that wait for printing and mailing or for external publication schedules. And because of the immediacy of this medium, users expect prompt response on the organization's part. Finally, some organizations become so enamored of the technology that they forget to match their Internet marketing presence with their true mission; while a Web page is a necessity for a national environmental organization with projects in eight states, it is not now the right medium for a low-income community policing group, all of whose constituents live in the same four-square-block area and where computer-based telecommunications penetration is limited.

Conclusion

A suggested hierarchy for Internet usage in a development office would have everyone using e-mail to communicate with volunteer leaders, key constituents, and colleagues; everyone would also have an understanding of list servers, newsgroups, and Gophers and other research tools pertinent to their functional positions and agency mission. Prospect researchers, proposal writers, and program developers would use research tools more extensively and they might also be regular participants (generating both inquiries of their own and answers to questions raised by others) in particular list servers or newsgroups. Organizations with appropriate outreach needs and the right target audiences would develop a Web page with appropriate links to pages at other sites along with an effective response apparatus.

When approaching any new technology, the new user must simultaneously understand its possibilities and its place in the current environment, master its techniques, understand its costs and risks, and make a decision for the organization or department that balances these factors. All it will take to turn a non-user to an "early-adopter" is a new development committee chairman who insists on e-mail as a day to day communications tool or a major local foundation putting its grant awards on-line the day after the foundation's board meeting. The presence of a competing organization on the World Wide Web will be powerful motivator for developing one's own page even if an environmental analysis shows that current usage would be low. And if reports of Internet fundraising change from their current uncertain result to truly positive, the pressure will be on to stake organizational claims in this new territory. When dealing with telecommunications, the wise decision maker looks beyond today's situation and tries to predict future reality—but he or she remembers that in this environment, the future may be only weeks away.

Resources

Worthwhile books about the Internet include:

Gaffin, A. *Everybody's Guide to the Internet.* Cambridge, Mass: MIT Press, 1994.

This introductory book is an expanded version of the Electronic Frontier Foundation's on-line "The Big Dummy's Guide to the Internet."

Krol, E. *The Whole Internet User's Guide and Catalog.* Sebastopol, Calif.: O'Reilly & Associates, 1994.
A comprehensive book containing pointers to a broad selection of Internet files and archives.

Heydorn, M. "Internet Resources for Not-for-Profits in Housing and Human Services." Published on line.
This is a downloadable Internet guide focused on nonprofit concerns (and more general than its title implies). It is available on the World Wide Web at:
> http://www.duke.edu/~ptavern/housing.html
It is also available via Gopher from University of Michigan libraries.

On HandsNet via their public forums:
> Using HandsNet
> Internet & Other Networks
> Expanding Your Internet Connection
> Internet Resources for Nonprofits

Here is a sampling of Internet resources of interest to fundraisers. Note that these are *case sensitive*—that is, the capital and lowercase letters in the titles and addresses do make a difference, and you need to enter them exactly as given here. Replace phrases in brackets with the indicated contents, without brackets.

1. Fundlist (list server)
   Audience: Primarily higher education
   E-mail to: listserv@jhuvm.hcf.jhu.edu
   Message: sub fundlist [YOUR FIRST AND LAST NAME]
2. prspct-L (list server)
   Audience: Primarily prospect researchers
   E-mail to: listserv@uci.edu
   Message: subscribe prspct-L [YOUR FIRST AND LAST NAME]

3. soc.org.nonprofit (newsgroup)

    Audience: General nonprofit management. Anyone
    with newsgroup access can read this newsgroup; steps to
    becoming a subscriber are different, depending on your
    Internet connections

4. Grant Getter's Guide to the Internet

    http://gopher.vidaho.edu:70/1s/e-pubs/grants

5. The Foundation Center (Web site)

    http://fdncenter.org

6. Sun Microsystems Community Development Grants Program
    (Web site)

    http://www.sun.com/smi/Corporate Affairs/grants.html

7. NPO-NET serves the Chicago nonprofit and philanthropic
    community and is an example of a locally-oriented Web site.

    http://www/mcs.net/~nponet

DEBORAH STRAUSS *is executive director of the nonprofit Information Technology Resource Center in Chicago, providing assistance with technology to nonprofit organizations. She is a long-term member of the National Society of Fund Raising Executives.*

There are many important issues to consider when selecting fundraising software—involving both the software itself and the organization that will use it.

5

The right tool for the job

Tim Mills-Groninger

FUNDRAISERS NEED the right tools to do their jobs well. Computers are an undeniable part of the tool set. The right software in the hands of a skilled fundraiser is a tremendous asset to any campaign or annual fundraising activity. The wrong computer system can be an expensive and frustrating hindrance to the advancement of institutional goals. Being able to tell the difference between appropriate and inappropriate software tools is an intimidating but very necessary skill for a development officer.

Too often, choosing software is considered a magical process. Selection is often deferred because the plethora of products (over three hundred fundraising databases have been released in the last ten years) paralyzes the staff member anxious to make the right choice. Well-meaning peers offer no end of conflicting recommendations and warnings. Board members wonder why a system can't be built from mail-order software in a weekend. Volunteers and consultants vie for the opportunity to help create a system. Through all of this, the development director is afraid that if she screws it up she will be fired. Yet there is also the hope that software can solve problems.

NEW DIRECTIONS FOR PHILANTHROPIC FUNDRAISING, NO. 11, SPRING 1996 © JOSSEY-BASS PUBLISHERS

Staff new to development believe that the donor management software can unveil the hidden mysteries of fundraising, or at least teach them their jobs. There is the hope that software will know to do things that have been overlooked. Like the Texan who didn't know about art, but knew what he liked, the newer fundraiser doesn't know what to ask for in fundraising software, but thinks that she'll know it when she sees it.

There's many a fundraiser who has never met a feature she didn't like. Fear, unease, lack of confidence, and other disorders are tied up in the selection of software. Many try to err on the conservative side and overbuy. If a feature isn't used, too bad, maybe my successor will have the time—I'm too busy trying to keep my head above water. While there is some merit to this approach, one fundraiser referred to it as "using a dump truck to go to the corner store—it'll get you there, but it won't be easy."

This chapter seeks to demystify the software selection process and reduce the number of options to more manageable units. Rather than reviewing specific packages or consultants as though they were so many new cars, it aims to help the fundraiser develop a clear idea of system requirements that can be used to compare the various options.

Asking the right questions

The number one question development officers have when they begin the selection process is, quite naturally: "What is the best fundraising software available?" Asking for the best software is like asking for the best glue: it depends on what you're doing. A glue stick is great for holding paper together, but I wouldn't use it to fix the handle of a coffee cup. Even narrowing the question to type of organization, such as social service or budget size, isn't enough to identify the right software choice.

Budget size is a poor indicator of need. In an extreme example, if three $250,000 annual donors provide your whole income, you won't need much in the way of software, although you may want to hire a couple of bodyguards to ensure your donors' well-being. But if you raise that same $750,000 from several hundred donors giving less than $100 each, your data management needs are significant.

To begin the fundraising software selection process, you'll need to answer questions in three areas: organizational profile and resources, donor profile and commitment, and development goals. Other questions will naturally follow, and quite rightly you may find yourself asking very fundamental questions about agency goals and the direction of the development effort before you start to look for the first flicker of a donor profile on a computer screen.

Organization profile and resources

What does your organization do and how is it organized? In the context of this chapter we assume that you know what you are doing as a fundraiser and that your message and ask are appropriate to your prospective audience. One organizational profile may be more appropriate for individual fundraising, another may best be suited for gifts from corporations and foundations. It's an obvious point, but many fundraisers in the quest for the perfect package overlook it. Organizational profile will determine the scope of the effort, and the mission will determine the message.

After mission, resources are the biggest determiner in specifying software. The most critical organizational resources are money, staff, and time. Even though fundraising software is a money-making product, return on investment is rarely a factor in its selection. Almost every organization has some limit that it cannot exceed. However, before shutting the door on higher-priced options, it is good practice to evaluate the long-term benefits of the most appropriate tool. Before the software selection process begins, you should be ready to determine the basic price range and the upper limit for first-year expenses. Remember, out-of-pocket financial considerations are only part of the equation, and the application of staff effort or an expanded time frame can save money.

Conversely, accelerating the selection process will increase the stress on staff and likely increase the financial outlay.

One way to look at the balance of resources is to imagine a pie chart of money, time, and staff as in Figure 5.1. A surplus of staff skills reduces the need for out-of-pocket expenditures. Reducing the time frame requires more staff or money.

The biggest single mistake a development officer can make is to do the first cut for software based on price. The next biggest mistake is to believe that the sticker price encompasses your major expense. The reality is that the cost structure of a development system is complex. In addition to hardware and software, there are major costs associated with implementation in the first year. If the goal of the new system is to significantly improve gift income, significant changes to the status quo are also required. Some degree of office reorganization is necessary, along with process review, training, occasional course corrections and general disruption of work. In simple terms, change is expensive. The good news is that expense isn't just measured in dollars.

Staffing is often an overlooked asset. The more skilled the development staff, the more understanding and control they have of the situation. Staff members with an interest in technology can create

Figure 5.1. The resource pie

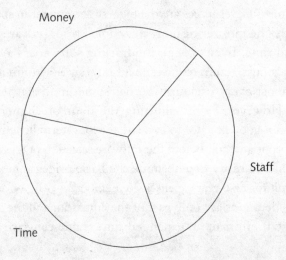

a development database using low-cost generic database software. Development officers with extensive skills in sales and negotiation may benefit from commercial sales contact tracking software to help them cultivate major donors.

Staff attitudes toward technology and teamwork, and overall staff experience, are all factors in determining the correct software solution. Technical skills, while a definite asset, are not a major requirement in system planning or selection. Common sense and a detailed knowledge of the operations and reporting requirements of the development office are much more important to the successful implementation of new (or improved) software. The most successful fundraising systems have staff who understand the business rules that guide the effort. Prepackaged software will impose some rules, and not necessarily the right rules for your situation.

Time, particularly when coupled with an organization's capacity for change (or at least capacity to withstand grief) is one of the most neglected resources. A stable development system with no impending crisis permits time to be spent lavishly on specifications and evaluation of alternatives. An impending major appeal with nothing organized is an invitation for missteps and errors. Time and staff effort are also needed to collect information about prospects and donors. A donor management system with lots of space for detailed dossiers on each donor is useless unless there are sufficient research and data entry resources to populate those fields.

Creating an effective development software system requires an understanding of financial limits and the ability to extend those limits through staff skills. Offices with less skilled (or, and this is more important, less motivated) staff will spend more money on a system than those where enthusiasm and energy are expended on the automation effort.

Development goals

Income is not always the critical factor in measuring the effectiveness of a development effort. Most businesses look at return on investment as a long-term goal, and that is certainly a valid measure in many development offices. In other fundraising efforts, long-term donor commitment and visibility in the community are more important than churning many small gifts in a short period of time. Development goals will affect how a system is used and how it changes the development effort. An agency that uses a development system as a way to facilitate community involvement, as we've seen with some community-based organizations, has different development goals from an agency that depends heavily on contributions from major donors.

Profiling your development system

Different software options treat data differently and provide unique ways to meet development goals. Knowing the profiles of your donors and the types of gifts and other exchanges you have with them will help you select a system that emphasizes those needs.

Databases classify the world into entities and transactions. Entities are the things, the subject of the sentence. A donor, the person who gives, is the most obvious entity in a fundraising database. Institutions can also be entities, as can families or other groups of people. Knowing just what entities you are likely to encounter will shape your database requirements. Transactions represent some exchange or action between your organization and the donor entity. Gifts are the most obvious transactions, but attendance at cultivation events, personal meetings, and other contacts count as well. Multiple values for a category, such as community affiliations, can also be considered transactions. Anticipating the potential transactions between you and your donor base will give you the information to make the right decisions.

Regardless of how entity and transaction information is presented on the screen, it is stored in a row and column format called a table. A table is a two-dimensional grid where each column represents a single characteristic or field and each row is an instance or record of a specific entity or transaction. Entity and transactions are linked by special fields called keys (Figure 5.2). Keys, usually in the form of ID numbers, play no other role than uniquely identi-

Figure 5.2. A simple donor database

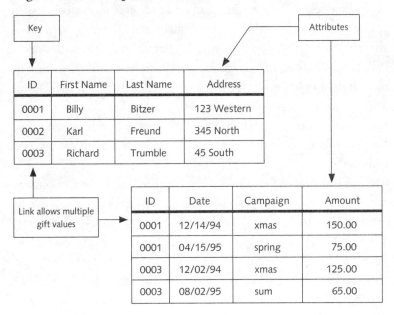

fying records to provide these links. The fields that actually hold information about the entity or transaction are called attributes. An individual donor record typically will have a single key field and upwards of two dozen other attributes that contain information about the person.

Fields can contain only one piece of information: a last name, an address, a phone number. When an attribute can contain multiple values, such as several phone numbers, you will either need to create more attributes (fields) or create a new transaction table. As you profile your development system, be careful to identify data elements that can be handled in a single field (gift date) and those that may require a table (relationship history).

Donor profile and commitment

Generally, fundraising software is thought of in terms of the centralized and coordinated solicitation of individual (sometimes called annual) donors, the majority of whom give one to three times a year in modest amounts. A small number of these individuals, called major donors, will give much larger amounts—the process of identifying, cultivating, and receiving large gifts from these donors is called conversion. Typically, prospects can be readily drawn in as annual donors because they feel a connection between themselves and the agency's goals and mission. Within the classification of individual donors, it is often necessary for the development office to track members of the same family, corporate relationships, and other affiliations.

Another class of fundraising involves the solicitation of philanthropic entities such as foundations and corporations. In approaching individuals, the agency calls the tune in setting deadlines, defining the appeal, and evaluating the effectiveness of each campaign. In soliciting institutional philanthropies, the donor calls the shots; where few individual donors will notice that the holiday appeal is two weeks late, most foundations will notice when a proposal is even a day late. Likewise, where the goal of individual fundraising is to be as nice as possible to the largest number of people through the crafting of a message that has a broad market appeal, institutional fundraising involves tailoring a message specifically to the interests of a single foundation, and sometimes even to the interests of a specific individual within that foundation.

Many organizations work with civic groups, congregations, fraternal organizations, and other associations of individuals as part of the fundraising effort. These clubs are often a major source of revenue. Some are, in terms of data management, very close to the profile of the individual donor. Each club is, for solicitation purposes, an independent entity, and will contribute as part of an agency-initiated campaign. Quite often, the campaign information is sent out in the same manner as a direct mail appeal, and follow-up is similar for nonrespondents. Other groups require the same sort of proposals as a private foundation. Still others require tailored presentations keyed to dates in the club calendar.

Understanding the donor profiles for your organization is important in selecting the right software. The right system will allow for the classification of donors appropriate to the solicitation effort and to the entity. Individuals are the easiest, but their giving levels are often modest. Multiple relationships between individuals and organizations are difficult to track, but for a development office that understands those relationships, the payoff can be substantial.

While data about donor interests and relationships are critical to creating successful campaigns, there is a balance between what you want to know (everything) and what you can afford to collect in database form. When identifying donor profiles you will need to weigh the value of certain information with the cost of gathering it. Doing extensive research on annual donors may not be possible. Many house lists consist of nothing more than name and address information, supplemented with the occasional phone number, because that is the only information available on the check.

Organizing your donors into the smallest reasonable number of classes provides direction for the development effort. Knowing that a part of your constituency includes families where several family members will make individual contributions means that the computer system should track family relationships. However, there is often a Catch-22 problem in which the current system lacks the sophistication to provide information necessary to determine the requirements for the new system. The only way to break this vicious circle is to do some research on suspected patterns among donors, to determine quantity and complexity. Finding patterns from a sampling of your current system is a good indication of how complex the conversion to a new system will be. Often there is a belief that new software will turn up new information about links between donors or other features. While this is true to an extent, it is also true that new packaging rarely improves old data.

Gift profiles

If donors would just recognize the importance of your agency and send you the money when asked, you could get on with your life. Unfortunately, donors require more options than the two-word solicitation, "Please give." The most common gift profile is unrestricted cash resulting from a direct solicitation. Over time, you will be able to predict with great accuracy how quickly and to what amount your list will respond to your requests.

Requirements for memorials, bonuses and incentives, in kind, and other giving methods have to be outlined as part of the planning process. Remember that while giving donors lots of options may seem like a good thing, keeping the process as simple as practical is the most advantageous. Limiting the giving options allows you to concentrate on the message, not on bookkeeping.

Pledges, those unconstrained promises to pay a specific amount of money over time, are an interesting database challenge. Frequently the donor's payment schedule does not match the promise, and there is a need to have an established policy to recognize irregular fulfillments. Some offices track overpayments of pledges as new gifts, others hold the excess to offset unfulfilled amounts. Restricted gifts, particularly grants, have special requirements, especially in reporting.

Campaigns

Solicitations are usually grouped into campaigns that provide a focus for the appeal and a means to measure the overall effectiveness of the effort. For some organizations, campaigns are little more than the mailing dates of specific appeals. For others, they evoke all connotations of a major battle with detailed strategies, commanders, objectives, rallying points. The broadest definition of a campaign is any coordinated contact with a set of donors or prospects. Using this definition, a campaign does not always receive gifts, but is nevertheless part of the cultivation process.

From a database standpoint, you should distinguish between campaigns that explicitly list all the contacts (that is, keep a list of everyone who received a solicitation, regardless of response) and campaigns that list only the results (the gifts received). In many situations, knowing a donor's profile and when the name was added to the list, you can determine which individuals were probably included in a particular campaign.

Database software options

With a review of development goals and a solid profile of donors and gifts in hand, you can begin to evaluate software options. Traditionally, there have been only three major options for creating a database system: hiring or training staff to create one from scratch—called do-it-yourself; contracting with an outside entity, volunteer or paid, to create a custom system; and buying a commercial off-the-shelf solution. Each choice has its own merits and pitfalls, and success relies heavily on staff, financial, and time considerations. Experience indicates that a database system of a given complexity will ultimately cost the same amount of money, the only question is how the funds are allocated.

Overview

Do-it-yourself systems involve only a small cash outlay for a generic database software package. However, the commitment of staff time to create the system is a major resource drain. In many agencies, the people who end up designing the system were not originally hired as software specialists. The usual pattern is that they had some development or administrative responsibility and drifted into software design because they showed some interest or affinity for the subject. Home-grown systems usually work best when they have modest goals.

Vertical market solutions are the software equivalent to buying clothes off the rack. If the fit is good, you've gotten a great deal. If there is only a limited correspondence between the original package and what your agency needs, the alteration costs will probably outstrip any advantages offered by the sticker price. When off-the-shelf solutions work, they provide agency staff the luxury of focusing on service delivery instead of software details. When they don't work, staff are forced through a series of software-mandated contortions to perform even the simplest chore.

Consultant-written applications tend to be quite complex. Usually paid by the hour, developers want to create as comprehensive a system as possible given the financial and time limitations. When done well, consultant-written systems create a custom fit for agency needs and allow the greatest flexibility for future growth. When done badly, they are a financial black hole of astronomical cost for negligible benefit. Trust and communication are the most critical factors in dealing with a consultant.

Surprisingly enough, the decision-making process for any solution is the same. The most critical component is to be able to describe the problem in plain English in light of the considerations of resources and profiles already discussed. Next comes an understanding of the situation at a macro level. The mechanics of the process must be clearly understood. Finally, it is important to set goals appropriate to the resources available. When the task at hand is understood at a mechanical level, staff are better prepared to evaluate the alternatives and select the best fit.

Ultimately, the costs for each are similar for development systems of the same level of sophistication. The graph in Figure 5.3 indicates the general trend comparing cost and complexity. The curve denotes the overall relationship of cost to overall sophistication, and the boxes mark the general boundaries for the different options. Note that costs escalate at a much higher rate than sophistication. Small increases in power can involve a major resource investment. Ultimately, you will reach that point of diminishing returns where even substantial increases in funding will not make the application more advanced. This trend is true not just for fundraising databases, but for other database applications as well.

Do-it-yourself or agency-built applications tend to be the simplest and consultant-written applications the most complex. Both options also have the potential to become cost-control nightmares, which is why they are plotted much wider than they are tall. Off-the-shelf applications tend to fall in the middle of the curve, where

Figure 5.3. System cost and complexity

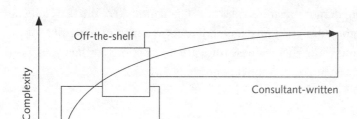

modest increases in cost can make the most difference in performance. Because the best developers are more experienced, costs are more predictable than with the other options.

Building your own database

Development offices with uncomplicated gift processing requirements and interested staff can successfully build their own systems. In the case of soliciting organizational entities, this may mean a sophisticated spreadsheet that tracks hundreds of proposals per year. For a staff-driven major donor effort, Personal Information Manager (PIM) software may provide the appropriate tools. Naturally, the most sophisticated vertical market solutions will have these features built in.

Where the major effort is focused on individual donors with an incidental or opportunistic major donor conversion component, a generic relational database built by staff is the right tool. In the early days of microcomputers, writing a donor management application required the skills of a techno-fundraiser. There were so many steps between requirements analysis and design that the person assigned to the job had to juggle an almost inhuman number of details. Modern relational databases, focused on end user systems development, telescope the process of implementing a design.

However, as easy to use as these systems are, they still require a strong design. Business rules and a data model are the key elements to a good design. The data model acts as a map or blueprint for the system, while the business rules are instructions for handling both common and exceptional conditions or tasks.

The data model

Regardless of the approach—do-it-yourself, off-the-shelf (vertical market), or consultant-written—it is important to have a good understanding of the data model for your fundraising system. One of the best ways to uncover the data model is to create a goals statement for the system from the organizational, donor, gift, and campaign profiles discussed earlier. The goals statement should contain all the major data elements and operational rules. A simple statement might start out as: "We want to manage our six thousand individual donors and their twelve thousand gifts each year. We will acknowledge any gift over $100 immediately with a receipt and thank-you note; all gifts will be acknowledged at the end of the year with a summary thank you. We usually have four major campaigns each year, but we want to double that in the next three years."

It is important for the goals statement to be in English. If it is something that everyone involved can contribute to and agree on, the technical details will follow. The goals statement should cover the donor profile, solicitations or campaigns, and gift processing. Typically, a first draft will be one or two pages.

From the initial goals statement, identify the major entities and transactions, and list the major data elements of each. The simplest donor system has two entities (donors and prospects, and campaigns) and a single transaction (gifts). Often, the system manages more than donors and prospects. Tracking board and committee members, volunteers, and other relationships can transform a donor system into a constituency management system. Adding a relationship transaction that lists the type of relationship and the beginning and ending dates can be a simple solution to this problem.

In the next step, take each entity and transaction and list its attributes. For each attribute, ask yourself if there is one value or many, and if many, the upper limit. For example, some development directors like to have two salutations—one formal and one informal. Those would probably be two fields in the donor table. Phone numbers, on the other hand, have multiplied for many people, and with voice, fax, car, pager, and others there may well be no upper limit. If it is critical to track each number, then you may need a transaction table to flexibly record all the possible variations.

Having identified data elements, check your work by creating sample reports on paper. It's not necessary to use a database for this, only to put the right information in the right place. If you find gaps in the reports, go back and add the missing attributes to the appropriate entity or transaction tables. At this point you have the basic requirements for the system, which can be used to compare consultant proposals with vertical market solutions or each other, or as a map for a system you create yourself.

When creating your own system, the next step is to begin experimenting with the database software. Create the tables and any necessary relationships and enter sample data. During the development process, it's a good idea to have a few dozen donor and prospect records that you are comfortable with. Sample data should reflect the diversity of the population you serve, and be familiar enough so that when you create a query or report, you'll know ahead of time what the result should be.

At this point, you're ready to start turning the database software into your development system. Start with the sample data to work out any technical bugs with the software. While a basic familiarity with your database software is required, you don't have to be an expert. With a good design and a clear set of goals, the technical challenges can be overcome in manageable units. The on-line help system and manuals give a solid foundation for learning the software. Third-party books, user groups, advice from volunteers and friends, and formal training courses are all good sources for learning more about the software. When seeking advice from volunteers and friends, remember that the goal is for you to learn more about software, not for someone else to create technical wizardry that you don't understand or can't repeat.

When you are comfortable with the software and confident that the core data entry and report components are working, it's time to start working with live data. If moving from another generic database program, you should be able to import the data in a few hours—depending on the design and quality of the information. When moving from a paper-based system, you're faced with the daunting task of data entry. As unattractive a chore as this is, it is also an opportunity to review your list in detail. Some records will be incomplete or contain information that is obviously inaccurate or otherwise odd. Developing a procedure to set aside questionable records during data entry will help to improve the overall quality of the list. Distributing responsibility for data entry among key staff and volunteers will make the work go faster, train future users early in the process, and provide feedback on the overall system. Because databases store data separately from data entry screens and procedures, there is always an opportunity to change the way things work without affecting data already in the system. Listening to user comments during these early data entry sessions can help create a system that fits the overall work flow of the office.

Once you have your donors and prospects in place, it's time to adapt the software to your campaign strategy. For most individual donor systems, this step involves the selection of prospects, production of labels and letters, and gift receipting. In the early stages of system development these steps are only partially automated. Most development officers select the entire list for the initial solicitation and export it to their word processing software for label and letter production. Word processing software has traditionally had two advantages over most databases. First, word processors have had better typographic and layout controls. Secondly, staff tend to be more comfortable with their word processors. While improvements in database software have eliminated the first reason, staff will likely always be more comfortable with their word processors. There is little technical distinction in choosing one approach over the other, and over time either can be automated to a very high level.

Gift receipting is entirely a database problem. Often a gift contains new or changed information about the donor, while the gift itself can change the donor's status, as with giving clubs. In individual systems, the goal is to record the gift quickly and accurately, but with the option of correcting information in the donor record as required. If the solicitation has a return piece containing name, address, and other vitals, along with the donor's ID number (key), then finding the record will be simple, and the donor can indicate any changed information. In check-only gifts, you're faced with a more complex task of searching for the donor by name, and—based on the results—determining if the donor is new or already in the system. Most databases have a phonetic search function that can aid in finding records where you're not sure of the exact spelling. Regardless of how the donor record is located, the gift entry screen should allow for editing of donor information, automatically record the donor's ID in the gift record, and provide default values for the most common gift amounts and purpose codes.

One process in use in many development offices is to have the accounting office open and deposit checks in daily or weekly batches. Response pieces and copies of the checks are then forwarded to the development office for data entry. The development office then runs a report summing the gifts for a particular batch. As long as the development office report agrees with finance office's deposit record, the system is in balance. In this type of arrangement, the finance department tracks income at the fund or purpose level and is relieved of the task of tracking gift details by donor. The development side of the operation can concentrate on managing donors, leaving the audit and other financial tasks to the finance office.

Gift acknowledgments are similar to solicitations. Record selection and response type are often based on gift level. Production of the acknowledgment piece, whether post card or merge letter, can be done within the database or via export to a word processor.

While technically feasible, printing acknowledgments immediately after gift entry tends to disrupt work flow, making another argument for working in batches.

Because screens and reports only affect how data is presented, not how it's stored, you can modify your gift processing system as you go without jeopardizing the integrity of existing data—assuming, of course, that the data model is sound and you are collecting all the information you need. If there are substantial structural changes required to the entity and transaction tables, you should stop all data entry and return to the design process as quickly as possible. If feasible, you should try to update existing records after the redesign to make the system as consistent as practical.

The final test of your donor management system is its reports. Depending on the sophistication of the database development, its accessibility, and staff familiarity with the system, the need for detailed paper-based reports may be minimal. The most popular reports are those that heavily summarize activity. Few people like to see a twelve-page listing of every gift received in the last six months, but a one-page listing of gifts by size, category, and campaign can captivate an entire office. In addition to the presentation capabilities of your database software, you can export data to a spreadsheet for further analysis and manipulation.

Developing an in-house database is an ongoing proposition, and as the world changes the structure and direction of your database will change. While the major development can be done on a part-time basis in three to six months or a year, you will never really finish the system; you'll just not spend as much time with it after it settles down. Doing it yourself can be a good option for situations when you're not too sure of what the system should look like, but think that it's probably simple. The process of profiling the system, developing goals, and prototyping the database will clarify many points and define many preferences. After a year, there will not be so much invested that you can't just transfer the data to a consultant-written or vertical market application. What's been learned in the application development process can also be used to evaluate other options.

Vertical market do's and don'ts

When evaluating fundraising software, it is important to use the organizational, donor, gift, and campaign profiles as a shopping list of features. The nonprofit trade press is filled with ads for software, and your profiles will be the only way to compare vendors' claims with your needs.

Choosing which products to look at can be a daunting task. If possible, talk to colleagues about their experience with particular vendors. Many publishers have developed niches in particular areas of the country or in particular types of agencies. Anyone who is already spending time in your area or knows your type of organization will have an advantage in servicing your account. Word-of-mouth referrals from people you know can help identify the better vendors. Referrals from people whose organizations you don't know can sometimes be misleading—particularly the negative ones. Our experience indicates that many product complaints come from organizations that failed to train staff properly or allowed their support contracts to expire.

Developing a relationship with the vendor is important. No matter how good the product or training, you will need regular access to technical support in order to use the product to its fullest. The most common vehicle for this is an annual support contract. One developer stated that the role of his company was to provide fundraising consulting services, and that they developed their software to make that process more efficient and economical. Moreover, support contracts also provide you with access to free or discounted upgrades to the product. Few vendors go more than eighteen months without issuing an upgrade, and often refuse to support versions more than two revisions old. Outside of the formal support arrangement, you should also feel comfortable enough with the vendor to be able to call about questions unrelated to support and not feel intimidated.

In evaluating the software, pay particular attention to how well the screens and reports match your profiles. You will rarely find an exact correspondence between your list of data elements and those of the program. However, you can often find software that "thinks" the way you do in general terms and where the logic of the system is similar to the way your office runs. Compromise is an important part of adapting a particular fundraising program to your office; go into the evaluation process with a good idea of features that are negotiable and those that are must-haves. In some cases the software's way of doing things may be better than what you had planned; in others, the program's approach will be totally unacceptable to the culture of your office.

Many staff spend too much time in making the final selection between the top two or three programs. No one can fully evaluate a program before working with it for six months or a year, so it may be unfair to expect anyone to make the perfect choice the first time. The reality of the situation is that fundraising software development is a highly competitive industry, and products at a certain level don't have a lot to distinguish them technically from one another. If a feature is in one product this year, it will probably be in the next release of the competition's product. If you're working with a publisher you can trust, you'll have everything you need in short order. If you find yourself in a situation where, for whatever reason, the software isn't working out, it is a fairly straightforward proposition to move your data to another program. Almost all the significant vendors have data conversion services designed to make it easy for you to move from some other database—including one you may have written yourself.

Because of the highly volatile worlds of development and technology, it is unrealistic to plan to be using a particular program more than three years. At that point, changes in hardware and your office will have made parts of your original plan obsolete. Your current vendor will have gone through one or two major upgrades, and you will want to do a cost-benefit analysis of upgrading, staying the same, or switching to a new program. Surprisingly, switching to new software can be very cost effective when spread over the three-year product life span. Fundraising software is a tool, and it is OK to change tools when it means you can do more work faster.

Concerning consultants

When used effectively, consultants provide all the technical sophis-tication of vertical market software (and beyond in many cases) and the customization of a self-developed program—without the need to sacrifice staff time on technical details. When used poorly, both the fundraising staff and the consultant are left ill-tempered, blam-ing each other, and over budget by three to five times the original estimate, and the software is apt to be buried under a pile of mis-understood specifications.

The key to effectively using a consultant to create your fundrais-ing database is communication. If the consultant can repeat to you what you've said in a way that indicates full understanding of what you want, you're well ahead of the game. Good consultants will recommend an interview process that mirrors the profile process described above. Doing the profiles yourself beforehand can con-sequently save some money because the consultant will not be start-ing from scratch.

While the consultant will want to talk with everyone involved in the development effort at least briefly, it's good practice to assign a staff member to act as liaison. In addition to coordinating the con-sultant's day-to-day activities, the liaison should be learning the consultant's overall methodology. This effort brings some of the consultant's expertise in-house, making the resulting software eas-ier to use and maintain. Understanding how the consultant works and what went into your software means that potential problems can be detected and solved earlier. The most common problem in developing custom software is that the client cannot express needs in terms that can readily be translated into the logical rules required for programming. The consultant in this situation creates a program that performs only the specified functions, not what was implied and understood by the client. There's an old joke among consultants: "The cruelest thing you can do to your clients is give them exactly what they've asked for."

Break the consulting contract into several phases, generally design, prototyping, programming, implementation and testing, and ongoing support. Establish milestones and deliverables for each phase, and specify that either party can terminate the contract at the conclusion of a phase with no penalty. If you've found that you've made a mistake, you get out easily and finish the project with someone else.

Remember that even small changes in the complexity of a project can mean significant cost increases. The only way to control costs is to develop realistic goals, stick to them, and work closely with the consultant to make sure the upper limits of the project are clear. Projects can be bid on a fixed-cost basis or on time and materials. Either approach is acceptable as long as the project is well managed. In situations where the consultant is not given enough supervision, the fixed-cost project gives him an incentive to finish quickly and provide only the stated specifications. In a time and materials situation the incentive is to add features and performance while increasing billable hours.

The contract should indicate ownership of the software. It is most common today for custom programming to be done on a work-for-hire basis, where your office is the owner of the program code. Some offices go into the software development effort believing that the final product will be so good that it can be sold commercially. Maybe it will—but if your needs are so much like the rest of the world's, why can't you just buy a vertical market solution?

Conclusion

Fundraising software is a tool. Like any tool, it is judged by how well it can do the job. Development offices can approach the job of fundraising a hundred different ways, and so there are a hundred different tools. They are not magical, they are not precious; they are just another part of a system that begins with the goals of your agency and leads on to that connection with a donor, however defined. The effectiveness of your fundraising software will not be in how popular it is, or in how much money you spent on buying or building it, but in how well it helped you establish that link with a donor.

TIM MILLS-GRONINGER *is the associate executive director of the nonprofit Information Technology Resource Center in Chicago, providing assistance with technology to nonprofit organizations. He is also chairman of the Technology Resource Consortium, a national network of computer technology resource providers.*

Technology can provide substantial assistance with prospect research, making prospect management more efficient and effective.

6

Computer-assisted prospect management and research

Laura J. Avery, John L. Gliha

J. C. ORDINARY, an alumna of the class of 1970, just called to say she will be on campus tomorrow and would like to meet with you. You've never met Ms. Ordinary but hope that her request to visit with you means there is a major gift lurking in the background.

You turn to your keyboard and retrieve Ms. Ordinary's biographical file. There's nothing there except an address and a giving record of $100 a year for the last ten years. It's time to move to cyberspace. You tap into the Internet, and within minutes learn that Ms. Ordinary is anything but. The founder and sole owner of an electronics firm in the first stages of an IPO, she appears to be worth $250 million. She has a condo in London as well as a home in Grosse Pointe, Michigan. She is an avid golfer, and her company has cosponsored an LPGA tournament. She is also a volunteer board member for several charities. Your hopes for that major gift soar.

A wonderful fantasy? At the moment, yes. Even with today's advances in technology, prospect research is not an exercise in instant gratification. There is much to be gained through the use of computers in terms of speed and access to certain types of data. However,

NEW DIRECTIONS FOR PHILANTHROPIC FUNDRAISING, NO. 11, SPRING 1996 © JOSSEY-BASS PUBLISHERS

the thought that the Internet will eventually access everything you need is probably unrealistic.

So what do you, as a manager, need to consider when establishing a research operation? How do you take advantage of the technology that is currently available to efficiently and effectively support a research operation?

Your primary considerations should be:

- What prospect information do we need?
- How quickly do we need that information?
- How do I allocate personnel resources for information retrieval?
- What financial resources are needed for start-up and ongoing operations?

The four fundamental questions that need to be answered before asking for a major gift are: Why might this prospect be interested in the organization? Who is the best person to cultivate the prospect and, ultimately, ask the prospect for a gift? When is the right time to make the request? What level of support should we be seeking from this prospect?

All your research efforts should be directed toward answering these questions. Much of the information you need will come directly from the prospect once someone affiliated with your organization begins developing a personal relationship. The minimum amount of information you need on a prospect is name, address, telephone number, and affiliation with your organization.

It would not be cost effective to build personal relationships with everyone in your database, so you will want to know whether or not the prospect is likely to be capable of a major gift. A quick but imprecise way to do this is to see if the donor falls within the top ten percent of all donors to your organization. This question can be answered by reviewing not only the size of the largest gift and lifetime giving, but also the frequency and recency of each donor's giving. You can also use some form of peer screening—have volunteers review lists of donors and identify anyone they think might be capable of a major gift. Or you can use any one of a number of computer-assisted prospect segmentation systems that we will discuss later in this article.

Once you get beyond this early prospect identification stage, you will begin the prospect qualification and research stage. Here you will be more interested in accumulating information about the prospect's interests, personal connections to your organization, personal assets available for philanthropy, and readiness to be asked for a major gift.

Your most important research assets are human, not technological. It is your responsibility to impress upon everyone, including volunteers, the importance of research and the four fundamental questions. Every meeting with every prospect and every research action should be aimed at answering these questions. Invest in teaching people how to be good interviewers and good listeners. Require everyone to complete call reports every time they interact with a prospect.

The information fed back to a prospect researcher after a volunteer or staff meeting with the prospect can save the researcher valuable time by pointing out prospect interests and personal connections. Details that might seem insignificant may be the clues the researcher needs to identify the right resources for determining wealth or personal connections with other prospects. This will also save institutional money by not wasting assets researching information that is already known.

While a great deal of information can be accumulated through personal contact with the prospect, you will still need a researcher. There are too many prospects and not enough staff or volunteers to build long-term relationships with everyone. Most small shops (those with fewer than thirty thousand constituents) should have at least one prospect research specialist. Hiring the right person to conduct your research and providing the right computer tools will greatly increase the efficiency and effectiveness of your fundraising program.

Your research specialist should be knowledgeable about on-line computer databases as well as print resources. Even if you choose to hire someone with no previous experience in *prospect* research, look for someone with experience in *on-line* research. On-line research time can be expensive if the researcher does not know the basics of how to focus database searches into the narrowest acceptable protocol.

Computer facility is not the only skill you should look for in a research specialist. You also want someone who is innately curious, is capable of critical and analytical thinking, has a well developed sense of ethical responsibility, and is a self-starter. The best prospect researchers understand the needs of development officers and volunteers. They will search for relevant information, not just gather data. They will help development staff members focus their prospect cultivation activities and play an integral part of the overall development process.

As a rule of thumb, an experienced prospect researcher using on-line research techniques can complete eight to ten prospect profiles per week. This is three times the output of a researcher using only print materials. Consider everyone in your development operation (including your chief executive officer) a research assistant. Everyone needs to be communicating everything learned about a prospect to the research department.

Basic office computer tools

For prospect research and management, you will need to invest in a good computer for the storage and retrieval of information. IBM-compatible hardware running DOS (and Windows) is the dominant development office equipment. You can find software for Macintosh and Digital equipment and for the UNIX operating system, but your choices are somewhat limited.

Ideally, the system in which you invest will consist of networked PCs. This will allow all development officers and researchers to transfer documents between terminals, as well as allow multiple access to the main database. You will have software that stores standard biographical and gift history data as well as software that tracks your prospect management efforts (and your office budget, campaign targets, and a myriad of other basic office functions). For research, you will also need a CD-ROM (Compact Disc—Read Only Memory) drive.

No matter what hardware and software decisions you make today, the rapidity with which technology advances assures that the next generation of equipment will be on the sales shelf the day your system is installed. Don't let that delay your decision. Just be sure that you are selecting systems that will meet your predictable future needs and are flexible enough to adapt to needs you may not anticipate.

Here are some of the questions you should be asking: Will your constituency grow modestly (5 percent to 10 percent per year) or are you looking for exponential growth over the next five years? How large a development staff will you have? How many volunteers will you be managing? How many prospects will you be managing? When will your next capital campaign begin? Do you need to be networked to the finance office? The admissions office? The alumni/ae office? The membership department? Will you need to manage major special events such as gala benefits or class reunions? Do you need special software for publications design?

Given the variety and complexity of software available for development use, you might be well served to spend the money to hire a consultant who understands your needs and can make recommendations on appropriate system configurations.

Your basic software supporting prospect research should cover all of the following basic storage and retrieval needs:

- Biographical information for primary constituent and family
- Detailed gift history to your organization
- Volunteer activities
- Event participation record
- Organizational relationships
- Data related to prospect's capacity and willingness to give
- Prospect management data
- Standard reports for fundraising targets
- Standard reports for prospect management

Special tools for prospect management

For purposes of this discussion, *prospect management* involves any effort to organize a constituency into smaller groups that can be more efficiently and effectively cultivated and solicited for gifts, and then tracking the progress of cultivation and solicitation. Prospect research involves efforts to understand specific attributes of an individual, thereby enhancing your ability to develop specific cultivation and solicitation strategies for that individual.

If you think of prospect management and research as an Oreo cookie, prospect research is the creamy filling, prospect management is the chocolate wafers. As with Oreos, some people focus more on the research filling than on the management structure surrounding the research.

But prospect management has an important role to play even before a specific prospect is assigned to the prospect researcher for in-depth information gathering.

Computer-assisted prospect segmentation

Whether you have ten thousand or five hundred thousand constituents; whether you have one researcher or ten; it can be a great advantage to have your file scanned by any of a number of commercially available computer-assisted prospect segmentation services. (See Resources index at the end of this chapter.)

One type of computer-assisted segmentation system scans your database and ranks all your constituents based on ability to give and philanthropic propensity. These systems generally append one or more codes indicating the relative likelihood that a particular prospect might be a candidate for cultivation and solicitation for a major gift. You then import these codes into your computer system and have an easy and efficient method for quickly sorting your total constituency into smaller groups based on potential to contribute large or planned gifts. Many of these services will also append specific data related to age, socioeconomic status, and demographic details.

Another type of computer-assisted segmentation will provide specific types of data on those individuals who match the vendor's database. For example, if the vendor database consists of individuals who own private aircraft, each individual in your file who shows up in the vendor's file will be flagged as owning a plane—a good indication of substantial resources.

Both types of systems can be tremendously efficient in sorting your total constituency into smaller groups from which you can isolate those individuals you believe deserve further research based on their raw, unqualified potential to contribute.

These systems provide one of the Oreo cookie wafers: they help you preselect the prospects you want to feed into the prospect research area.

Computer-assisted prospect tracking

The other wafer consists of computer-assisted prospect tracking of researched prospects who are assigned to staff or volunteers for cultivation and solicitation. All the information gathered through computer-assisted prospect segmentation and most prospect research will be easily stored in your basic information management software. But you need a simple method of identifying and monitoring progress on prospects whom you believe able and willing to make major gifts.

Make sure you include in your software requirements fields for storing codes that indicate a prospect's position on the solicitation staircase illustrated in Figure 6.1. No matter what the size of your constituency, you want to be able to separate those people who are closest to solicitation from those who are one, two, three, or four steps away. This may be as simple as a letter code that is regularly updated by you and your staff, or it may be a sophisticated coding system based on a statistical model that is updated by the computer whenever certain pieces of information are added in key fields.

Figure 6.1. Solicitation staircase

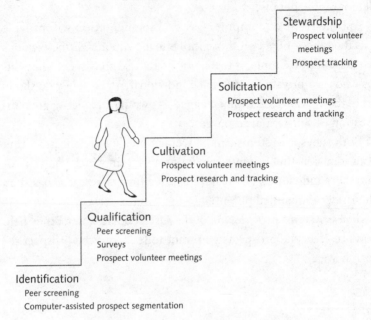

Stewardship
Prospect volunteer
meetings
Prospect tracking

Solicitation
Prospect volunteer meetings
Prospect research and tracking

Cultivation
Prospect volunteer meetings
Prospect research and tracking

Qualification
Peer screening
Surveys
Prospect volunteer meetings

Identification
Peer screening
Computer-assisted prospect segmentation

There are several prospect management software systems available that can assist you in moving prospects up the solicitation staircase. (See Resources index at the end of the chapter.) All of them provide means for tracking prospects, staff, and volunteers and their interactions. These systems produce reports indicating who is assigned to whom, what the last contact was and when, what and when the next contact will be, and various other pieces of information needed to ensure that you, as the manager, know whether your program is moving forward or standing still.

If you think you are too small for a computerized prospect tracking system, think again. Although routinely called *prospect* tracking systems, these systems track staff and volunteer efforts as well. Remember, you need to be planning for the future, and even if you don't envision your organization growing exponentially, your ability to manage staff and volunteers in any major fundraising effort will be greatly enhanced by using prospect tracking software.

Special tools for prospect research

Not all prospect research can—or need—be done through computers. Many of the hard-copy reference materials your researcher needs may be available at a local library or you may be able to establish a share arrangement with other local nonprofits. However, many reference resources are available on-line and you should be ready, willing, and able to access them.

Beyond the basic computer setup, your researcher will need a modem and a dedicated phone line. Invest in the fastest modem available. Modem speed can save you money when downloading data from any of the on-line databases available to your researcher.

On-line resources

To begin your on-line resource library, consider the services offered by DataTimes and Knight-Ridder Information, Inc. DataTimes provides full text access to over 1,400 regional, national, and international news sources including newspapers, wire services, and magazines. They offer an overnight clipping service where you can retrieve in the morning any mention that has been made of your organization (or certain prospects) in any of the DataTimes news databases worldwide. You can also get business reports with corporate profiles, securities transaction information, and other key financial indicators.

The Knight-Ridder Information, Inc., retrieval service, formerly operating under the name of Dialog, was established in 1972. It contains over four hundred different databases, indexing more than 320 million records. This retrieval service covers a broad range of disciplines; the individual databases are maintained by separate companies. Like DataTimes, Knight-Ridder, Inc., serves as the middleman, providing you access to multiple databases for a set sign-up fee ($295 as of April 1, 1995). Access and searching through individual databases will be charged at a rate set by the various vendors maintaining the databases (costs average $70 per hour). (See Resources index at the end of the chapter.)

Finding lost constituents

Over time, every organization loses some of its constituents—they move, change their names, just get lost. There are several services available to help you get reacquainted with your lost constituents.

In 1986, the U.S. Postal Service established the National Change of Address (NCOA) database. Several vendors are licensed to provide change of address information using this database. Generally, you send a computer disk or tape containing the last known address of your constituent and the vendor will return a tape or disk with new addresses for found constituents.

Some companies have specialized services for finding lost constituents by accessing the NCOA database as well as large marketing databases and credit reporting agencies. Many of these companies can work without the constituent's social security number, but they are all less expensive if you have the SSN. The service fees vary by vendor and the size of file you want to search, but you can count on a minimum of $1 per name.

Budgeting

How much will you need to invest to have a computer-assisted prospect research program? Exhibit 6.1 gives a brief overview of factors to consider in a fairly small research office budget, and the rest of this section goes into more detail.

Obviously, a great deal depends on how much computer hardware and software you already have. Let's assume that you have a basic development computer system that can manage your constituency database. Beyond these basics, you will need to consider the cost of:

- Personnel
- On-line resources
- CD-Rom drive
- Maintenance and upgrading of computer equipment
- Specialized software for prospect tracking
- Computer-assisted prospect segmentation
- Print resources

Personnel

Salary and benefit costs for a prospect researcher will vary somewhat depending on geography and the experience of the person
you hire. Count on spending anywhere from $20,000 to $30,000
in salary for a researcher with some familiarity with on-line research techniques. Add your organization's benefit package and you
will have a ballpark figure for initial budgeting purposes. How
many researchers you need will depend on the size of your organization, the number of major gift officers each researcher will support, and the size of your next capital campaign.

There is no magic formula for determining the exact size of your
research staff. Many campaigns for $100+ million function well
with as few as four researchers, while some institutions elect to have

Exhibit 6.1. Research office budget

Personnel	$25,000/researcher
Print resources	$700–$7,000
On-line resources	$100–$200/profile
Prospect segmentation	$6,000–$12,000
Hardware	
CD-ROM	$ market price
Modem (high speed)	$ market price
Telephone line	$ market price
Software	
Prospect tracking	$ vendor
Professional development	$1,500
Basic office support	
Telephone	
Supplies	

Note: These figures assume an office with fewer than thirty thousand constituents.

a ratio of one researcher for every five development officers. Most organizations with fewer than thirty thousand constituents, or modest fundraising goals, function well with one full-time researcher.

On-line resources

Again, there is no standard dollar amount on how much you will spend in this area. On-line services generally charge on a per-hour basis for the time you are actually connected to the service; these hourly charges can vary from $20 to $200. Many also charge an annual access fee. You will need to come up with some estimate for your first year in operation. Afterwards, that you can use the previous year's expenses to extrapolate future costs.

One way to do this first-year estimate is to set the number of profiles you want completed in the first year and estimate $100 to $200 for on-line costs per profile. Keep in mind that on-line resources will represent anywhere from 40 percent to 60 percent of your total resources budget.

CD-ROM drive

Some of the information you will be looking for is available on compact discs called CD-ROMS. Many new computers come equipped with a CD-ROM drive for reading these discs, and an external CD-ROM drive can be purchased separately and attached to most computers. The kinds of information available on CD-ROM include a telephone directory combining all U.S. white pages, a zip code directory covering all U.S. addresses, the Martindale-Hubbell directory of U.S. attorneys, and several Who's Who directories. The cost of CD-ROMs varies and may drop in the near future but you can expect to pay $200 and more per disc.

Specialized software

Prospect tracking software can be as inexpensive as a standard off-the-shelf spreadsheet package (EXCEL, Lotus 1-2-3, or similar programs) or database management packages (dBase, rBase, and so on).

The problem with using these types of software is that only the initial purchase is inexpensive. You will then have to spend time developing and maintaining your own tracking system within the framework of the software. Therefore, it is worth the investment to purchase one of the specialized software packages. These systems were developed with your needs in mind and have been tested and improved through years of operation in various development offices around the country. Fees vary and you need to talk directly with vendors to ascertain your budget for initial purchase of this software.

Computer-assisted prospect segmentation

Again, you will need to talk directly with vendors to determine your costs. When considering this type of segmentation, remember that your investment will be repaid in two ways: you will reduce the time needed to find major donor prospects and, depending on the type of service you purchase, you may reduce research time on many of these prospects. Fees for these segmentation services generally depend on the number of constituent records you elect to match against the vendor database, and costs may start at about $6,000.

Print resources

As wonderful as computers are, they can't do everything. Your basic research library will still need some resources that, to date, are only found in print. Your print library budget will depend on how many resources you share with other local nonprofits or are found in your local library. Sharing and using libraries does have a hidden cost in the time your researcher must spend away from the office. A basic print library can cost as little as $700 per year or as much as $7,000.

Computer maintenance and upgrading

Most computer maintenance costs will be covered under the basic service contracts you will purchase from vendors. However, you should talk to your software vendors about their history of producing upgraded software. How often do they improve their product? What have they been charging to upgrade their customers' software? Be sure to verify these claims with other customers. Use this data to budget regular upgrading of software.

Ethical considerations

In the excitement of the variety and depth of information that is available from on-line and print resources, it is especially important to consider the ethical issues surrounding prospect research. Our need to know is never greater than the prospect's right to privacy. There are four basic principles that should govern all prospect research efforts:

- *Confidentiality is non-negotiable.* Nonpublic information about a donor or prospect should be maintained in such a way that the relationship of trust between the donor or prospect and the organization is affirmed. Dissemination of information relating to a prospect should be restricted to those within your organization who have a need to know.
- *Accuracy is the highest priority.* Whenever possible, data should be verified by at least two reliable sources.
- *Gather only relevant data.* Only information that is relevant to the furtherance of your organization's mission should be gathered.
- *Data collection should be professional, responsible and in compliance with applicable legal practices.*

Your job as chief development officer is to ensure that you and your staff have the necessary tools to efficiently raise the funds necessary for your organization to fulfill its mission. You will need high-quality prospect research to effectively manage a successful fundraising program. By appropriately employing the technology available, you and your staff can quickly find the relevant data you need, manage that data in a confidential and respectful way, and maintain each donor's trust in yourselves and your organization.

Resources index

Prospect management resources

Prospect segmentation

ELECTRONIC SCREENING® with POTENTIAL PLUS®, Marts & Lundy, Inc., 1280 Wall Street West, Lyndhurst, NJ 07071. 800-526-9005.
Full file segmentation with prospect identifiers and additional data codes.

PROSPECT PROFILE™, Grenzebach, Glier & Associates, Inc., 211 West Wacker Drive, Suite 500, Chicago, IL 60606. 312-372-4040.
Full file segmentation with prospect identifiers and additional data codes.

PROSPECT SELECT, Bentz, Waley, Flessner, 5001 West 80th Street, Suite 201, Minneapolis, MN 55437. 612-921-0111.
Full file segmentation with prospect identifiers and additional data codes.

Prospect tracking

VIP Plus prospect tracking software produced by DataPlus, Inc., 4545 42nd Street, NW, Suite 209, Washington, D.C. 20016. 800-388-8340.

Gifted Memory™ prospect tracking software produced by Institutional Memory, Inc., 559 Solon Road, Chagrin Falls, OH 44022–3334. 216-247-2957.

On-line prospect research resources

Knight-Ridder Information, Inc., 3460 Hillview Avenue, Palo Alto, CA 94304. 800-334-2564.

Access to over 400 databases and particularly strong in business disciplines. Provides some full text access. Below is a sample of databases most often used by prospect researchers.

- *Biography Master Index:* Biographical citations on over two million individuals.
- *Dun & Bradstreet Million Dollar Directory:* Address, financial, and marketing data on over a 100,000 companies with net worth of $500,000 or more.
- *Foundation Directory:* Describes over 3,500 foundations with assets over $1 million or making grants of $100,000 or more annually.
- *Foundations Grants Index:* Information on grant awards from 1973 to the present by over four hundred U.S. foundations. Data updated monthly.
- *Grants Index:* Information on local, state, and federal grants. Data updated monthly.
- *Magazine Index:* Cover-to-cover indexing for over five hundred U.S. and Canadian magazines with full text available for fifty magazines. Coverage by title from 1973 to present.
- *Standard & Poor's Register—Biographical:* Personal and professional data on over seventy thousand key executives affiliated with public and private companies with annual sales over $1 million.
- *Who's Who in America:* Biographical profiles of prominent individuals.

DataTimes, 14000 Quail Springs Parkway, Suite 450, Oklahoma City, OK 73134. 800-642-2525.

Full text access to over five thousand news sources. Business reports available through *Executive Reports*. Nightly searches by organization or prospect names through *Private Eye*.

Dun & Bradstreet Business Information Reports, Dun & Bradstreet Information Services, 461 From Road, Paramus, NJ 07652. 800-933-3867.

On-line business reports regarding number of employees.

Insider Trading Monitor, CDA/Investnet, 3265 Meridian Parkway, Suite 130, Ft. Lauderdale, FL 33331. 800-933-4446.

On-line service to track stock transactions by corporate insider traders and banking executives.

DAMAR ON-Line Real Estate Information Services, DAMAR Corporation, 3550 West Temple Street, Los Angeles, CA 90004. 800-873-2627.

Provides real estate property values for select areas in certain states.

Compact D/Sec and Disclosure/Worldscope, Disclosure, 888 7th Ave., 44th floor, New York, NY 10106. 212-581-1414.

CD-ROM database with information on U.S. public corporations (Compact D/SEC) and seven thousand foreign companies (Disclosure/Worldscope).

Lexis Public Records, Lexis-Nexis, a division of Mead Data Central, Inc., 9393 Springboro Pike, P.O. Box 933, Dayton, OH 45401. 800-543-6862.

Contains various public records including real estate assessments and deed transfers for thirty-one states and corporation and limited partnership filings for fifteen states.

Lost constituents

Executive Marketing Service, 500 E. Shuman Blvd., Suite 300, Naperville, IL 60563. 800-367-7311.

Telephone look-up service for telemarketing industry.

Trans Union, 555 W. Adams Street, Chicago, IL 60661. 312-466-7773.

Print resources

A = Basic references (approximately $700)
B = Foundation center reference collection (approximately $500)
C = Additional references if budget allows (approximately $6,000)

A All local social registers, city directories, telephone books, news-papers, magazines, membership and donor rosters available in your area.

A Foundation Center. *Foundation Directory*. New York: Foundation Center, published annually.

A Glossbrenner, A. *How to Look It Up Online*. New York: St. Martin's Press, 1987.

A National Center for Health Statistics. *Where to Write for Vital Records: Births, Deaths, Marriages and Divorces*. Washington, D.C.: U.S. Department of Health and Human Services, National Center for Health Statistics, 1984.

A Standard & Poor's. *Standard & Poor's Register of Corporations, Directors and Executives*. New York: Standard & Poor's.

A *The American Prospector: Contemporary Issues in Prospect Research*. Rockville, Md.: Taft Group/American Prospect Research Association.

A Wright, J. W., and Dwyer, E. *American Almanac of Jobs and Salaries*. New York: Avon Books, published annually.

B Foundation Center. *The Associates Program*. New York: Foundation Center.

B Foundation Center. *The Foundation Center Reference Collections*. 5 vols.: *New York; San Francisco; Washington, D.C.; Cleveland; Atlanta*. New York: Foundation Center.

C Dun & Bradstreet. *Dun & Bradstreet's Reference Book of Corporate Management*. Parsippany, N.J.: Dun & Bradstreet, published annually.

C Dun & Bradstreet. *Million Dollar Directory: America's Leading Public and Private Companies*. Parsippany, N.J.: Dun & Bradstreet, published annually.

C Economist. *Who's Who in the Securities Industry*. Chicago: Economist, published annually.

C Gale Research. *Biographical Dictionaries and Related Works*. Detroit, Mich.: Gale Research, published annually.

C Gale Research. *Who's Who in Technology*. Detroit, Mich.: Gale Research, published annually.

C International Biographical Center. *International Who's Who of Professional Business Women*. Cambridge, England: International Biographical Center, published annually.

C Marquis Who's Who. *Index to Marquis Who's Who*. Wilmette, Ill.: Marquis Who's Who, published annually.

C Marquis Who's Who. *Who's Who in America*. Wilmette, Ill.: Marquis Who's Who, published annually.

C Martindale-Hubbell. *Martindale-Hubbell Law Directory*. Summit, N.J.: Martindale-Hubbell, published annually. (Also available on CD-ROM.)

C National Register. *Directory of Corporate Affiliations*. Wilmette, Ill.: National Register, published annually.

C National Register. *Macmillan Directory of Leading Private Companies*. Wilmette, Ill.: National Register, published annually.

C Taft Group. *Owners and Officers of Private Companies*. Rockville, Md.: Taft Group, published annually.

C Taft Group. *Taft Corporation Giving Directory*. Rockville, Md.: Taft Group, published annually.

C Taft Group. *Taft Foundation Reporter*. Rockville, Md.: Taft Group, published annually.

C Wind River. *Directory of Women Entrepreneurs*. Atlanta: Wind River, published annually.

LAURA J. AVERY *is a vice president of Marts & Lundy, Inc., a fundraising consulting firm based in Lyndhurst, N.J.*

JOHN L. GLIHA *is a senior consultant with the same firm.*

High-quality reports stem from good data collection, excellent communication, and awareness of fundraising objectives on the part of the individuals who prepare them.

7

Reports and report generation that effectively support a fundraising organization

Pamela J. O'Neil

REPORTING AT MOST ORGANIZATIONS is unique to the culture and individuals in that organization. However, the types of reports that are requested and useful fall within three general categories: reports needed for individual programs; reports needed to assist in measuring and evaluating the progress of overall fundraising efforts; and reports used for public information or public access. Every organization, large or small, relies on and needs all these reports.

Valid, reliable reports that can be routinely generated are developed by combining the expertise and knowledge of several individuals. Individuals interested in viewing a report need to communicate with those who maintain and acquire the data, and both parties need to work with the computer technical support in defining and identifying the specific internal processes and procedures that will result in accurate reporting. A colleague recently pointed out to me that neither the staff nor the computer are clairvoyant; therefore, a great

NEW DIRECTIONS FOR PHILANTHROPIC FUNDRAISING, NO. 11, SPRING 1996 © JOSSEY-BASS PUBLISHERS

deal of communication and teamwork go into producing valid and reliable reports.

Why is it that good reports are so difficult to produce?

Reporting requires that someone in the data-collection and maintenance area know exactly what type of information the fundraising staff is interested in receiving. For example, a survey sent to all your organization's supporters may include several questions about interests regarding specific programs of your organization. Your data-maintenance staff is only interested in the address and phone number updates, and—not realizing the importance to the fundraising staff—they never key the other information into the database. In this example, any future access to the program-specific information provided by your supporters would involve going back through all the surveys and manually identifying those who had a specific interest. If, however, the data maintenance staff were aware of the importance of this information to the fundraising staff, they could code and enter program interests at the same time they were updating the address and phone information. Later, when a question is raised as to which individuals expressed an interest in a specific program, the information could readily be retrieved from the database. While the initial processing of the surveys becomes more complicated and time consuming for the data maintenance staff, future questions that will support the fundraising staff can be answered in a more efficient and timely manner. Obviously, individuals working with data collection and report generation must have a good understanding of current and future fundraising goals in order to provide effective support to the fundraising process.

Most of the databases we currently work with in a nonprofit organization were originally intended to record and receipt gifts and produce mailing labels. In more recent years it has become necessary for our databases to have a more integrated marketing focus. Higher-education fundraising and some medical fundraising organizations have had close to two decades of working with a database designed with a marketing focus. However, even in these more technologically advanced organizations, many continue to have report generation problems.

Reports for individual programs

Each program area is interested in tracking the success of its own fundraising efforts. The annual giving appeal looks at how many new donors as well as repeat donors made a commitment during a given solicitation. Fundraising event program managers need to know the net proceeds of their events, the necessary follow-up calls, and the quantity of pledges that were obtained. Comparative information reflecting the growth of the program over the past years and projected goals for the future must also be available. To manage an area effectively, a manager must be familiar with reports relevant to necessary decisions. The challenge is to make sure that the necessary information is gathered in such a fashion that it is easily accessible to end users.

Reports have always been produced at the program area level. Often it is because the person who takes the reservations or receives the gifts manually tallies the information. However, regardless of the reasoning for their production at the program level, if this information is collected in an isolated manner, the flexibility of the data will be severely hindered. Unfortunately, the piecemeal introduction of technology in many organizations has fostered this sort of isolation. When developing a reporting system, it is important to focus on making information easily transferable.

Transaction processing—our beginnings

Most databases in a nonprofit organization were designed to record and receipt an occurrence or an event. For example, a gift is received, a piece of mail comes in with a new address, or a phone number is discovered. Each of these individual occurrences is generally handled as an independent change or transaction. As we consider what information is relevant to collect and maintain for our organizations, accounting needs are frequently addressed first. Most organizations easily move the gift recording and receipting function from a manual process to one that has all the information housed in a computer. Since the processes are repetitive, this is a predictable first use of computer technology. However, transaction processing, or treating each item of information that is important to the organization as a separate entity, can create a narrow view of the data gathered.

If information gathered from a fundraising event includes names and addresses of those attending the event, this information can sit as isolated data and be separate from the lists of past contributors or volunteers who are also involved and committed to your organization. As long as we look at each functional area of our organization or each transaction as being an independent process, then our reports are limited. For example, to answer the question: Which people at the event have been past supporters or volunteers? may require acquiring a list of supporters from the gift processing area and a list of volunteers from the volunteer coordinator, and manually comparing them with a separate list of attendees gathered at the event. Another alternative is to rely on the memory of a long-term staff member. However, many nonprofits have found that staff turnover is too high for effective long-term memory to develop.

Limiting our thinking to isolated functions in the organization and viewing them as unrelated entities produces reports that become useful only after many hours of manually comparing information retrieved from isolated data-gathering sites. Reports can only reveal the information that has been consistently and accurately collected over time.

Frequently, the names and addresses of an organization's donors are maintained separately from the names and addresses of the organization's volunteers or of the best public relations contacts. In this environment, the work flow that keeps these groups separate has been carried over into the computing environment, and the problem of names appearing on more than one list continues to haunt the organization. Sometimes the names are not even easy to compare because of differences in the way they have been stored and maintained. For example, one work area may always enter names as a last name followed by a comma and then the first and middle names, while another work area enters names as "Mr. & Mrs. John Doe" and is only interested in viewing the names in zip code order. We find in each organization that some of these historic differences have kept areas functioning independently even after computing databases are introduced. Differences in data storage in an organization hamper effective reporting. If compromises leading to uniformity cannot be made in data storage, then the outcome is less accurate and timely report generation.

It is possible to successfully generate reports within organizations that maintain their information in separate databases even when there are stylistic differences embedded in one database. The fundraising staff can find out who has made a gift or even who made a gift last year but not yet this year. So, fundraising can continue.

The major weakness of a separate database environment becomes apparent when management-level reports are needed. When working to identify the success of all program areas—the fundraising receipts, volunteer utilization, attendance, and success of special events—several different reports are necessary. It is also much more difficult to identify the individuals who are involved with multiple functions of the organization. It will again be necessary to obtain several lists and manually compare by name to see if someone is involved as a donor, a volunteer, a ticket purchaser, or a sponsor of an event. Additionally, stylistic differences within one database mean reports simply never appear clean—for example, if names are formatted differently and abbreviations are used inconsistently, the columns won't line up in an orderly fashion.

Management-level reports that are a composite of separate reporting streams are very rarely useful for identifying and assisting in planning program area priorities. For these purposes, a marketing information system is needed, one that goes many steps beyond simply housing all your data in one database. The information gathered should support efforts to define future markets and interested audiences for your organization's cause and not simply report on the successes of past efforts.

Measuring and evaluating overall fundraising progress

Where is your organization headed? Is there sustained interest in your cause? Are you successful in recruiting and retaining volunteers and donors or are you constantly working with the same pool of volunteers? These are all questions that should be answered in order to evaluate the your organization's future opportunities.

Developing a marketing information system

Designing a database so that there is one location to look up information on anyone who is connected to your organization and so that all activity regarding that supporter is attached to this record resolves many issues. By utilizing one name and address for each donor, event attendee, ticket purchaser, volunteer, or committee member, an address update is complete after being recorded one time. Additionally, differences in how a name is stored are resolved by establishing consistency at one entry point instead of attempting to coordinate entry across several different program areas. But the greatest benefit is found in report generation.

The generation of mailing lists is simpler when a one-entry-per-individual design is in use. There is no longer the need to guess how many final labels will be generated once duplicates are removed. The tedium of comparing lists to identify multiples going to the same address is eliminated. This ease of label generation reduces the frustration all staff feel in regard to accomplishing their primary responsibilities of fundraising, event planning, volunteer coordination, or ticket sales. When our simplest needs are supported, then everyone becomes more optimistic about the possibility of accomplishing more sophisticated reporting tasks.

The ability to work with a comprehensive report assists work flow. If my fundraising questions are answered after accessing information at one place one time, I will approach the entire reporting process positively.

If the database design has a constant focus on how to best support the mission of the overall organization, then a marketing information system can be developed. Too often, enhancements or developments made to information storage after the initial computerization are in response to isolated needs. The computer experts making the changes, whether employees, outside consultants, or volunteers, generally are not aware of overall organizational goals. It is expedient in the short term to convey only the current needs of the current project to these individuals. However, without knowledge of the overall organizational goals and future needs of all program areas on the part of the computer experts, data collection and storage will continue to be developed as disjointed and unrelated parts.

The organizational mission of a nonprofit is not to create the best-ever database design. It is to advocate the social, religious, medical, or artistic goals it was organized to promote. With a solid basis of information designed with the overall objectives of the organization as the guide, you will find that the information provided supports your efforts the majority of the time. I have not yet seen any system in any nonprofit organization that is a 100 percent solution to each program area's current and future needs. However, a 100-percent-solution goal will keep the information support staff focused on your organization's needs, even though changing environments in technology and in the nonprofit itself mean the goal is always one step out of reach. On the other hand, recognizing that the perfect information system is always going to be unavailable, do not allow program areas or staff to limit their productivity based on the excuse that the information isn't on hand yet. Much philanthropic good continues to be done without the most recent technology.

Reports used for internal planning

Often I hear the statement, "We have a great database and we seem to be capturing information consistently, but I still can't get the reports I need." Defining reports that are useful and work well for your organization is not a one-time task. As the questions that generated the original report are answered, many subsequent questions come to mind, and these new questions can't be answered based on the original report. The fundraising knowledge of the individual responsible for generating your reports of goals and objectives will assist at these times. Often, if more time is spent in developing the original report, then subsequent questions can be answered more easily.

Understanding how the people who will use reports perform their work also helps in designing good tools for them. For example, a fundraiser asks for a report listing all the individuals who made a contribution last year. It is a simple process in most organizations to generate this listing. If, however, the person responsible for generating the report took the time to ask, "What are you intending to do with this report?" the actual report generated may more effectively meet the final needs. If the response is, "I intend to use our word processing software to send a letter to those people who gave over $200," this additional information allows the person generating the report to indicate whether the audience of $200+ donors can be directly loaded into a merge document in the word processing software. The result is many hours of labor saved by the fundraiser.

The data that we collect in a nonprofit organization is potentially our most powerful tool. However, the data must be turned into usable information through the reporting process to realize this potential. It is only possible to develop a truly useful tool if communication lines remain open.

Reports for future planning

Another class of reports is needed by fundraising staff to assist in their personal work efforts. These reports fall into two categories.

First are those reports that track or help plan work efforts. There are many software products available that help to track the productivity and contacts of individuals in the sales industry. This is the type of software that is most useful to fundraising staff.

The questions that a good sales management or contact tracking tool should be able to answer for the fundraising staff include: Which individual, organization, or foundation needs a follow-up visit or contact this week or month? Who has traditionally made a gift this month but is not yet heard from? Which pledge payments do we anticipate this month and have the appropriate letters or reminders been sent? Which donors or prospects are likely to show up at a community meeting that fits into a staff member's travel schedule? Which dates are critical for grant proposal submissions and what are the dates when we expect to hear of award decisions?

Fundraising has occurred for many years with all these questions successfully answered by people who kept very accurate calendars. With the proliferation of computers, especially laptops, the desire to automate these functions and merge the information with existing reporting streams became very strong.

The second type of reporting helpful for fundraisers includes accurate information regarding progress made toward goals that have been established in the fundraising plan. The information provided should answer the following kinds of questions: How many donors have responded? With how much money? How many pledges still have an outstanding balance? Who has given and are we successful in upgrading giving levels?

The generation of reports needed by individual fundraisers was perceived by many organizations as less of a problem as staff became personally proficient users of computers. Individuals could design and create the report tools they preferred. However, this short-term solution has several drawbacks. First, a fundraiser who spends hours mastering the computer and designing report output is not focusing on implementing the fundraising plan. Second, if each function within the organization or area designs and develops its own reporting mechanism, are the reports comparable and compatible? How will standards be determined? Third, is the information from different assignment areas being shared effectively?

The next step—decision-support systems

Thus far we have discussed developing and maintaining a well-designed, accurate, and uniform database to help decrease drains on the labor force. However, unlike other tools that reduce human labor, a well-used computing system can do more than simply record, reduce, or replace. To fully appreciate what computing technology can do for an organization, it is necessary to expand our view of database technology from a simple filing system to a tool that helps us efficiently use our organizations' resources. This is the concept behind what is commonly referred to as a decision-support system.

Decision-support system (DSS) is simply the name given to taking your data manipulation to another level—from mere collection to a management resource. A DSS is an organized collection of staff, databases, and procedures used to aid in making decisions. This process can be quite complex and intangible and is best explained by application. Take, for example, an organization that receives a large number of gifts during its annual drive, all of which need to be processed at the end of the year. The organization also has another operation that processes all preparatory operations (that is, mail, publications, data entry, and so on). Further imagine that both of these processes are carried out in separate departments that track their labor demands separately. By developing uniform recording processes, an organization can easily integrate this information with very revealing results. You may find that the two offices operate best separately. However, you may find that the two departments' peak workloads and downtimes run opposite one another. In this case, the two offices would benefit from being combined, since the labor pools are idle at different times. Either way, data has aided management in making a better decision.

This example allows us to see the potential benefits of unifying data internally. The next step is the combination of internal with external data—the benefits from which are nearly limitless. For example, we can now perform such complex analysis as regressing giving volumes against economic variables to model future giving! It is surprisingly easy to find the information to do such analysis— and even more surprising, much of it is free.

Public information and published reports

Each organization wants to be able to publicize its successes and compare its effectiveness with its peers. To do this, reports are produced and made public. However, as many within the non-profit sector will agree, we do not necessarily publish reports that are comparable. For example, do we report number of donors or number of donations? Do we record all outstanding pledges as collectibles or have we factored in a nonpayment rate? Each organization makes decisions on these questions that may be inconsistent with other organizations. As a result of this, any future decisions or goal setting based on how your organization compares with its peers may be problematic. When comparing or benchmarking your organization with its peers, it is first necessary to make sure the data are comparable. Fortunately, the incomparability of data among nonprofit firms may some day be overcome. Currently, many nonprofits are working toward standardizing their information and the result is a more comparable data set from which to benchmark. Additionally, it is important that the individual making external reports be aware of these standardizing efforts so that they too can include easily comparable data.

What information should be shared with your volunteers, boards, or committees? This question is raised frequently and needs to be defined and answered at the highest levels of your organization. Once management has formalized what information will be made available, a policy that helps both volunteers and staff understand this information and how best to use it is critical to an organization's success. Also, it is important for an organization to have clearly defined policies in this area to avoid leaking confidential information and losing the confidence of supporters.

Conclusion

Producing reports from databases and applying other computing technologies to support fundraising efforts can be accomplished if a few basic concepts are understood and followed.

- Reports are only as reliable as the information used to generate them.
- Consistency in maintaining information throughout the organization aids in timely reliable report generation.
- Use reports and reporting tools in the planning and evaluation for your organization. Management decision-making processes can benefit from identified trends and projections.
- Reports intended for internal and external use should be defined separately. Program area and management reports should also be designed to satisfy different needs.
- Your report generation staff need to understand and be involved in the fundraising goals of the organization. The more these individuals are personally involved in fundraising, the greater long-term value your reports and database designs will have.

A great deal of information is easily accessible even to the smallest shop; however, the key to successfully answering simple questions and modeling reports to answer more complex ones lies not in the volume of data collected but rather in its consistency, reliability, and relevance to your organization.

PAMELA J. O'NEIL *is the director of alumni/development information services at Ohio State University.*

Index

Ordering Information

NEW DIRECTIONS FOR PHILANTHROPIC FUNDRAISING is published quarterly in Fall, Winter, Spring, and Summer and is available for purchase by subscription and individually.

SUBSCRIPTIONS for 1995–96 cost $62.00 for individuals (a savings of 30 percent over single-copy prices) and $88.00 for institutions, agencies, and libraries. Please do not send institutional checks for personal subscriptions. Standing orders are accepted. (For subscriptions outside of North America, add $7.00 for shipping via surface mail or $25.00 for air mail. Orders *must be prepaid* in U.S. dollars by check drawn on a U.S. bank or charged to VISA, MasterCard, or American Express.)

SINGLE COPIES cost $22.00 plus shipping (see below) when payment accompanies order. California, New Jersey, New York, and Washington, D.C., residents please include appropriate sales tax. Canadian residents add GST and any local taxes. Billed orders will be charged shipping *and* handling. No billed shipments to post office boxes. (Orders from outside North America *must be prepaid* in U.S. dollars by check drawn on a U.S. bank or charged to VISA, MasterCard, or American Express.)

SHIPPING (SINGLE COPIES ONLY): $10.00 and under, add $2.50; to $20.00, add $3.50; to $50.00, add $4.50; to $75.00, add $5.50; to $100.00, add $6.50; to $150.00, add $7.50; over $150.00, add $8.50.

DISCOUNTS for quantity orders are available. Please write to the address below for information.

ALL ORDERS must include either the name of an individual or an official purchase order number. Please submit your order as follows:
   Subscriptions: specify series and year subscription is to begin
   Single copies: include individual title code (such as PF1)

MAIL ALL ORDERS TO: Jossey-Bass Publishers, 350 Sansome Street, San Francisco, California 94104-1342.

Previous Issues Available

NEW DIRECTIONS FOR PHILANTHROPIC FUNDRAISING